MARCH 26, 1988

Partners in Love

We have been and always will be Partners in Love. I will love you always.

Gene

ALSO BY DR. ELEANOR HAMILTON
Partners in Love: **First and Second Edition**
Sex Before Marriage
Your Engagement and New Approaches to Intimacy
Sex With Love

Partners in Love

Lovingness, Sex, and Communication in Marriage and Relationships

THIRD EDITION, REVISED

by Eleanor Hamilton, *Ph.D.*

SAN DIEGO • NEW YORK
A. S. BARNES & COMPANY, INC.
IN LONDON:
THE TANTIVY PRESS

© 1961, 1968, 1980 by Eleanor Hamilton

All rights reserved under International and Pan American Copyright Conventions. No part of this book may be reproduced in any manner whatsoever without written permission from the publishers, except in the case of brief quotations embodied in reviews and articles.

For information write to:
A.S. Barnes & Company, Inc.
P.O. Box 3051
La Jolla, California 92038

The Tantivy Press
Magdalen House
136-148 Tooley Street
London, SE1 2TT, England

Printed in the United States of America

Library of Congress Cataloging in Publication Data

Hamilton, Eleanor, 1909-
   Partners in Love.
   Sex in Love and Marriage

   Includes index.
   1. Marriage. 2. Sex in marriage. I. Title.
HQ734.H2585   1979   301.42'7   79-51018
ISBN 0-498-02431-8

3   4   5   6   7   8   9   85   84   83   82   81

to my partner in love

Contents

Introduction	9
1. Love Relationship Needs Two Loving Partners	15
2. The Development of Lovingness Part One: The Birth of a Loving Person	20
3. The Development of Lovingness Part Two: Oral, Anal, and Genital Affirmation	27
4. The Development of Lovingness Part Three: Givingness, Sharing Feelings, the Need for an Image of Love	33
5. Filling Up the Cup	40
6. Dissolving the Blocks to Lovingness	50
7. Communication in Marriage	62
8. The Wall of Moodiness	79
9. Sexual Artistry	94
10. Relieving Female Sexual Inadequacy	109
11. Relieving Male Sexual Inadequacy	122
12. Pregnancy: Planned and Unplanned	132
13. Money: Coin or Curse	147
14. Facing Up to Family Influence	158
15. Work for Both Partners	176
16. Religion in Marriage	188
17. Wayside Shrines	195
Appendices	211
Index	223

Introduction

As a marriage counselor, I listen every day to couples who tell me of their struggles to find joy in marriage. Somewhere deep in each of them is the hope that the marital relationship holds a promise for the *ultimate* in human happiness. Yet all about them they *see* failure, *feel* failure, and reap the results of failure based on ignorance, not intent.

As I work with them we talk of love. For the most part, we share the conviction that love *can* transform and illumine life; that it *is* a radiation outward that can be perceived even physically by anyone coming into its orbit; that its glow *is* warming and health-giving; and that from it *are* born most of the good feelings and creations that make living worthwhile.

Yet nearly every couple who comes to me comes needing *education for love*. Their relationships presumably based on love, need skillful partners in the art of loving, But who has taught them anything about that art? And who could imagine persons approaching any other adult task so ill-prepared?

I was lucky in my marriage. From the very beginning, I found a mate who, hand in my hand, searched out with me the little-known pathways to love's fulfillment. Moreover, our eyes were opened by a few courageous souls who saw what others had not yet seen and who dared to speak of what they saw. To researchers like Havelock Ellis, Robert L. Dickinson, Alfred Kinsey; to poets like Kahlil Gibran, Rabridranath Tagore, James Stephens; to the patient labors of many inspired psychologists, we give thanks for the enlightenment and freedom of *our* marital happiness. These men supplied the *keys* and we the *will* to unlock the doors to our own capacity to love.

Today a great deal is known about love that wasn't even guessed at fifty years ago, let alone acted upon. Marriage can be a song rippling joyously into eternity or a plunge into hell; an adventurous partnership in love or a boring imprisonment in the bonds of matrimony. What you make of it depends upon your willingness to *unlearn* everything that inhibits your capacity to love and to *learn anew* all that the artists and scientists of love can teach you.

In my own counseling office, there are only a limited number of consultation hours a week, and even then I spend endless time teaching *each* couple what must be taught to *all*. Over and over again, I share what I know of the art of love, helping each partner to break through his or her own resistance to loving.

It is true that this often requires the professional skill of a marriage counselor; but I am convinced that many partners in love could learn a great deal on their own if they were given the essential clues and if they could develop a point of view based on knowledge of cause and effect.

These clues and this point of view I have tried to put into the present book. When a friend of mine read the manuscript, she exclaimed, "Why! it seems to me that you are writing about a romp in the cradle instead of a roll in the hay!"

I was delighted, for she had given me the earthy words I wanted to state a principle upon which I find that committed relationships *can* succeed.

Introduction

"Exactly!" I chuckled. "One needs a romp in the cradle in order to mature to full enjoyment of a roll in the hay. The *kind* of romp, and the means whereby adult partners-in-love *can* make up for lost time, *is indeed* the thesis of this book."

My husband said, "The days that make us happy make us wise." This was his way of acknowledging the natural law that every healthy human creature reaches toward light and warmth. His own rare ability to act upon it, however, was what made *our* partnership in love a continuing joyous adventure.

My personal hope for you who read this book is that you will find here some clues to help you bring more light and more warmth into *your* partnership in love.

Partners in Love

1
A Love Relationship Needs Two Loving Partners

Partners in love expect their relationship to sprout from the seeds of love, as indeed it should, but perhaps they do not reckon that it can be maintained only if nourished by two loving people. This would seem elementary, yet few couples who walk into marriage today do so with a well-developed capacity to love.

While we pay lip service to the God of Love, repeating "Love thy neighbor as thyself," nevertheless, our tender regard for *ourselves* may be so undernourished that what little is available for another human being reflects our own starvation.

A minister said to me recently, "A half-filled cup cannot runneth over." He was giving voice to the principle that no one can give away that which he does not have. Like the cup, a half-filled person has no surplus to give; yet loving is giving.

Actually, the civilized world has never experienced the principle of love functioning as the law of life. The commandment to love is as revolutionary today as it was nineteen centuries ago. What the world has lived by, and taught its children to live by, is the principle of vengeance, springing from the loins of fear. "An eye for an eye, a tooth for a tooth" still prevails as the way we behave even if not the way we believe. This is not a humanly fulfilling diet but a punishing and depriving one. As a result, most of us grow up not only emotionally half-starved, but defended against the painful perception of our own starvation. What is more, we walk into marriage and other supposedly long-term committed relationships thus unfulfilled and thus armored.

"Falling in love" is a first step toward "being in love." It is the motivation from which couples can gain the strength and courage to scale the grander heights of enduring love.

Following are questions any couple might consider when they ask how they can determine the presence of love that is sufficiently strong to withstand the obstacles that arise in any normal marriage. Here they are addressed to the woman, but the criteria apply equally to the man.

"Do you feel good with him? Comfortable all over? Does your body long to fit into the curves of his body as if it belonged there and was eager to 'come home'?"

"Do you like the smell of him? The sound of his voice? The sight of him—including his fatness or thinness, his tallness or shortness, his ruddy freckles or olive tan. Do you like him with his lisp, his limp or his loping strides, with his manners and mannerisms, just as they are?"

"Do you like his character, his habits, and his behavior, without covert thoughts of changing these after you are married?"

"Can you feel joyous as you imagine yourself rendering him primitive personal services, in illness or in health, such as bathing him, easing discomforts, and rubbing his back?"

Does the thought of creating and nurturing a child between you fill you with deep ecstasy?"

"Do you find yourself sharing your thoughts and feelings with him, and being comfortable about it?"

Love Relationship Needs Two Loving Partners

"Do you cherish his well-being as deeply as your own? Can you let him move as a free spirit moves, helping him to seek his own way and his own work, without pressure from you? Or do you have a fantasy lover in your mind which, like a cloak, you wrap around your actual lover so that when he moves outside its confines you are threatened? Can you really let him BE?"

"Can you hear criticism of him by others and not be unnerved by it, yet not be deaf and blind to what you have heard?"

"In all the big and little affairs of life, is there an awareness of his Being that you carry with you, making you joyous as you discover ways of giving to him? Do you find your thoughts and fantasies taking off from and winging their way back to him wherever you are or wherever he is? Is he central, pivotal to your life?" And lastly, do you yourself feel liberated to fulfil your own life purpose?

I have learned from the sad experiences of distressed couples that those who say to me, "I never really loved him," are almost hopeless subjects for the resolution of difficult marital problems; but those who can say, "Once upon a time, we were passionately in love," usually offer the marriage counselor something substantial and basic to work with, once misunderstandings are out of the way.

Marriages can be good marriages without this kind of love; that is, they can be good, steady work vehicles for carrying the burden of responsibility for the world's job of maintaining homes; but they never transform the lives of the participants, never light up their eyes with the glory of love. For love resides in the heart of the lover and is known by its overwhelming desire to *give* not to *get*.

Too often, in my experience, partners will for a brief time bask in the pleasure of "being in love" and then become bitterly disillusioned when the bud of promise yields no fruit. Some lovers stand helplessly by, apparently without resource, permitting their love to wither and shrivel away. Yet this is the moment when they most need to understand the requirements of love's growth; for with such knowledge and the will to apply it, they are not so much without resource as they may think. Like a well-tended plant whose roots have been free to dip deep into rich soil their relationship must receive the nourishment it needs for productive survival. This nourishment can come only from two loving partners!

Unhappily, lovingness for most of us was seriously injured before we were six years old, often before the age of conscious memory. These injuries cause the emotional deficiencies that plague lovers and create a contest between two personalities instead of a partnership in love.

The difference between people who can love, enjoy, reach out, give, and accept and people who are blocked in these respects goes back, in all probability, to their differing experiences in early infancy. You, yourself, to be specific, no doubt react as you do today in a love or sex relationship largely as a result of your own experience as an infant, loved or not loved, responded to or merely "taken care of." You are not likely to recall, at this late date, your own infantile longings and fulfillments or frustrations. But by considering the kinds of things that *may* have happened to you during your first months and years of life, you may be helped to an understanding of your present ways of responding. You will thus be in a better position to offer your partner what is *now* needed to grow in a capacity to love, and, in turn, to accept what *you* need.

The missing elements that each of us required as children to grow in love are sometimes called by psychologists "unconscious needs." Their fulfillment was vital to the child, and the adult still unknowingly strives for their satisfaction. These are really nothing more than the aching voids, the suppressed longings carried over from childhood into adult life. When we understand them, accept them, and satisfy them in some constructive way, our adult capacity to love is increased and we are able to move onward into more and more enriching forms of loving.

Marriage offers an unusual opportunity for two adults to make available to each other those very elements which each needed as a child in order to grow in love. To help another "fill the cup of life" while having one's own cup filled is quite an achievement, but not at all impossible. It does require that you know how love develops in children, for only then will you be able to recognize your partner's unconscious needs and have the courage and inventiveness to fulfill them in the present.

Men and women who can offer such gifts to each other are preparing the soil for mature love, are planting the seeds of mature love, and will eventually reap a crop of mature love.

2
The Development of Lovingness— Part One: The Birth of a Loving Person

As you read this chapter and the next two, try to think in terms of the baby you yourself were, rather than of some other baby you know—the baby you have had or may have.

The baby you once were was constantly subject to feelings in motion (emotion). You became warm and expansive as you experienced pleasure, became cold and contracted as you experienced pain. Even *in utero* you were already subject to the results of the expansion and contraction of your mother. Perhaps you were held tightly by the unyiedling abdominal walls of a rigid and cold mother, or you may have been allowed room to move by the flexible walls of a warm and receptive mother who enjoyed your presence and her life.

The baby experiences communication on the level of sound and pressure. There is also some evidence that a baby can respond to those stimuli. A fetus can be sick or well, nourished or undernourished, accepted or rejected, with results that may be more shattering than similar experiences after birth.

In the actual giving of birth, the mother who is happily anticipating the coming of her child and who is educated and relaxed in the process is able to labor more effectively than the woman who is not so fear-free or so educated. The involuntary muscles of the frightened or resisting mother behave like powerful forces opposing each other. The result is pain, sometimes so serious as to impede the baby's passage into the world.

On the other hand, the involuntary muscles of the confident woman who is educated for birth contract and relax in so synchronized a manner that normally she does not experience unbearable pain. Her baby has a maximum amount of oxygen and is born with a minimum of trauma. Because it has been a relatively comfortable birth, the baby is not "all knocked out" from the passage. Already that child has a better impression of life. The mother can welcome her baby more wholeheartedly because she, also, is not so traumatized.

There is some evidence that words a new mother hears in the first moments after birth act as hypnotic suggestions that may influence her feeling about what she has produced. Research along these lines is still tenuous, requiring a great deal of further documentation. However, thoughtful doctors are beginning to watch what they say in the mother's presence when she is coming out from and going under anesthesia. It has been well demonstrated that words register, influencing the unconscious, even when the body is anesthetized.

For example, a doctor may say jokingly, "What a monster!" as he or she helps a healthy nine-pound baby into life. The "unconscious" mother hears, in a literal way, not perceiving his meaning. When she "awakens" she suffers a gnawing anxiety that all is not well with her child.

"Is he all right?" she asks her doctor, worriedly, if not with terror. All the reassurance in the world may not totally erase the sneaking suspicion that she has somehow produced "a monster," and this attitude is conveyed by her to the child.

I recently counseled with a beautiful and intelligent girl of twenty-three whose anxious question throughout her life had been "Who can love me?" The record shows, among other things, that when her grandmother had entered the birth chamber she had said to the new mother, "I'm glad that that isn't my baby. Who could love such an ugly mite?"

I make no comment about the effect of such a statement on the mother, but I do record it in the light of the girl's subsequent feelings about herself. We know that the story was repeated to the girl often enough to become engraved on her consciousness and to serve as an autohypnotic suggestion, conditioning her self-perception.

The evidence is overwhelming that the general attitude of approval or disapproval in the environment affects the baby's self-feeling.

When we are approved, our body tends to function without stress, naturally, easily, pleasurably. When we are disapproved, the reverse occurs. We tighten up (contract); our vital functions are interfered with and we experience physical distress in one form or another: constipation, colic, spasms of the throat, or, later on, inability to come to fully pleasurable orgasm.

The baby depends on its environment for good feelings about the self. If deprived, a child grows to manhood (or womanhood) needing unusual amounts of approval from a mate in order to feel welcomed and loved, confident of personal goodness and worth.

The baby reaches out to the environment for the satisfaction of all his vital needs. The first reach is for the air

The Birth of a Loving Person

needed to maintain life. The next reach is for food. If it is forthcoming from a loving person, the baby is satisfied, perceiving the world as good, as giving. If the baby fails to find what is needed, there are tears.

A baby of high energy potential does not give up without a battle. His crying reactions convert to rage reactions, and later on to the well-recognized tantrums of the toddler or perhaps to physical symptoms of a dramatic and acute nature. His or her unfulfilled "reach" has met with frustration. Frustration may be expressed as anger. Expressions of anger may, in turn, bring this child punishment or isolation (severe punishment). ("Let the baby cry it out," advises the unpsychiatrically oriented doctor).

Rejection in any form brings fear of reaching. When we fear to reach, the result is restriction of movement with inability to ask for or to express love. A child thus learns to brace himself or herself against feeling and, later on, even fails to recognize the feeling. When a grownup encounters experiences which trigger off these early and painful unconscious "memories" of reaching that person is left with an involuntary tightening, perceived as a gulping in of breath and a muscular tension, usually a tied-up-in-knots feeling. Gradually these tensions become chronic in grownups. They are plainly visible to the eye of an expert, and even inexperienced persons notice and react to them.

A baby of low energy potential may simply give up, even to the point of apathy. Just a fraction more energy would help the child become the "good" and docile infant who will spend most of the time sleeping. Later on, as a child and grownup, that person will be the one who senses life as futile, often giving up before beginning.

On the other hand, the baby who "reaches" and receives learns that the world is responsive to needs. His or her reach has found satisfying response, and thus encourages the baby to reach again. This baby behaves differently from the unresponded to, unsatisfied baby. The child's disposition is shaped differently. Learning to expect fulfillment by reaching out, thus is associated with success, satisfaction, pleasure, with expansion.

Contrast him with the baby who reaches and doesn't find, or reaches and finds a breast reluctantly offered or a bottle held by a mechanical "baby-tender," neither of which could assuage the hunger of warm body contact, even though giving milk. For this baby, reaching is associated with pain, with desolation, with helplessness, with body contractions.

At the marital level, the problem of inability to reach, or fear of reaching, is so persistent that it represents one of the major problems brought to the marriage counselor. Presently, I shall discuss some of the ways that people in love can dissipate this fear, but first let us understand its origin.

Again observe the baby.

The breathing of the responded-to infant is different from that of one not responded to. It resembles that of a contented puppy's panting, where emphasis is on exhalation, not inhalation. Because the baby exhales fully and with total body mobility, without prolonged diaphragmatic contraction, all the waste matter is expelled and thus the oxygen intake is at its maximum, so the child is nourished by oxygen, which converts to a fuel, and thus to energy, as well as by food. Is this part of the answer to the riddle of contented babies who maintain nutritional well-being on very little actual food, quantitatively?

Let us further examine this matter of breathing, for it relates to such important matters as sexual functioning and the communication and release of feeling of partners in love.

In human life, the intake of breath is identified with the building up of tension and outgo of breath is identified with the release of tension. If you want an impressive demonstration of this, observe how you draw in your breath with a frightened gasp at a scary movie. While fear is experienced, you continue to limit your breathing to the barest perceptible movement and your chest is held stiff and high. When the movie is over, you exhale with a deep sigh of relief. Your chest descends and your abdomen expands.

So it is with all of us. With every exhalation that is not held in by accumulated tension, there is a pleasurable impulse that travels from the center of the body to its periphery. It can be perceived as a kind of wave, or current of pleasure, moving over the abdomen, through the genital area, down the legs and arms, and into the fingers and toes. This is the breath of life, of love, of pleasure. When we breathe like this, we feel alive. In fact, we "feel." We are open to deep and tender communication with all of living life. We have a sense of well-being and relaxed awareness.

But what happens to us if, as babies, we met with lack of response or with coldness or hostility in our environment? The baby, like our adult at the scary movie, takes a deep, gasping breath, sucking in air and holding it, releasing it only long enough to gulp in another. Very early the baby learns to contract against feeling his own anxiety and scare-aches. The expression of longing is often denied, which is illustrated by shallow breathing or holding a breath.

As an adult s/he is limited in capacity to perceive the feelings of others. S/he braces against sensing personal loneliness, lack of warmth, or hunger, because reaching out for the satisfaction of these needs has been too painful. Thus, in a sense, s/he becomes chronically contracted against pleasurable feeling also, and chronically afraid to reach. This is called, by some psychologists, "pleasure anxiety." It is a deeply persistent problem in marriage.

Such an individual is easily identified. His (or her) body is not warm and yielding. It has become encased in a kind of immobilizing strait jacket, a rigid cage instead of a moving frame to house a mobile being. Breathing is shallow, energy flow is inhibited, and the observing eye of an expert can find in his or her body where the inhibitions lie. One of the first tasks of the marriage counselor is to discover these and to help the individual to release them. In a later chapter, I will indicate some of the ways that this can be done.

3
The Development of Lovingness— Part Two: Oral, Anal, and Genital Affirmation

All human beings are born sexual beings, and they remain sexual beings all the days of their lives. When sexual feeling is injured or blocked, the person, at whatever age, feels dead, uncreative, bored. Sexual energy is one of the wellsprings of creative life, and each of us feels good to the extent to which we are able to function creatively.

The tiny baby that was you discovered early, sometimes as early as the first few days of life, that genitals were a source of pleasure, providing good feelings about the self. We call genital explorations of this kind "genital play." If, instead, they are disparagingly labeled "masturbation" (meaning "to pollute with the hand") by a misguided adult, and if, perhaps, these words are accompanied by a slap on the hand that touches, then something which has been simply pleasurable is converted into something anxiety-ridden and fearful. In addition, the baby's good feelings about the self are injured. His or her sense of self-worth is harmed. This is what the psychologists call a "negative conditioned reflex."

To some extent, most of us in our culture are the victims of this indoctrination (conditioning). It is one of the reasons why it is so difficult for us to feel good deep down about our own genitality. Long after our minds have accepted the fact that guilt and shame are senseless and burdensome in a love relationship, our bodies retain the results of faulty and damaging conditioning. Many persons in positions of authority, such as doctors, clergymen, teachers, are themselves the victims of the scary admonitions relating to genital touching and, in turn, pass on their groundless fears.

Parenthetically, let me state here (and I will affirm it again when I discuss the art of sex) that if any of you are still struggling with this conflict, it might help you to know that the most reliable investigators have discovered that there are no harmful effects to a child or to anyone else from "playing with" himself or herself and finding sexual pleasure therein. On the contrary, they have found that genital play, (auto-eroticism), particularly where carried through to orgasm, helps to prepare the way for responsive, fully functioning, unblocked expression of the orgasm at its ecstatic best. In addition, it safeguards against premature, exploitative sexual relationships in adolescence or hasty marriages entered into almost exclusively for sexual reasons. Later on, it can provide release from tension in marriage or out of it when a partner is absent or indisposed, or when there is a wide disparity of sexual need. Finally, when death has claimed one partner, it helps the remaining one to endure the abrupt cessation of years of loving contact with a mate.

Returning to our infant, we observe that sucking is one of the first of its needs. We have noted earlier that it is also almost the first way a baby reaches out to life for satisfaction. Through the lips and the tongue and the throat, he or she takes in pleasure as well as food. The mouth is an erogenous zone. To the infant, it is the primary erogenous zone. When a baby is allowed to fulfill his or her sucking needs, a feeling of fulfillment pervades and the child moves on to satisfaction of other needs. If he or she is deprived of sucking enjoyment, that is, if sucking time is limited, for example, to that allotted to imbibe an eight-ounce bottle of milk, the baby may feel deprived. What is more, an attempt is made to make up for the deprivation by sucking a thumb, or blanket; in fact, anything that can be stuffed into the mouth. If interfered with in these activities by disapproval, he/she may start to bite, instead. The soft reaching for pleasure, as expressed in sucking, when frustrated, often converts to the anger reaction of biting.

A general principle to remember, not only in this situation but in others, is that whenever the outgoing reach of an individual is stopped in the fulfillment of a healthy, primary need, the reach turns to a rage. (Shakespeare was giving voice to this principle when he said, "Hell hath no fury like a woman scorned.") If the rage is punished, then eventually both the reach and the rage are repressed, and the individual suffers immobilization of feeling.

Look at the lips of the people you know. How many of them are drawn in a tight, repressed line, expressing no feeling whatsoever? Where and how do you suppose they "got that way"? And the jaws that grind in the night, holding back the rage and the bite; what of them?

Some psychiatrists feel that our excessive eaters and smokers may be acting out their need to fulfill themselves on this very earliest level of oral satisfaction.

The need to have the mouth loved and "given to," is reflected in the intense satisfaction most people get in having their mouths caressed and kissed. Particularly in our undernursed United States many men seem to crave the pleasure of mouth on breast of the woman they love! This brings me to say that we should give more attention to mouth satisfactions for our undernursed women who have no breast to turn to in adult life.

Proceeding to another matter, there is ample evidence that countless thousands of us owe our sex shames, sex tensions, and sex guilts to premature or compulsive toilet training. A whole field of medicine, proctology, serves a steady flow of patients with rectal and anal complaints. Another field of medicine, psychiatry, spends endless hours attempting to undo damage done to the psyches as well as to the somas of their patients.

To the baby, a bowel movement is an act of pleasure and creation. "I made it!" the baby crows. It has, after all, come out of his or her body. It feels good. If mother smilingly receives it, approving baby, the baby feels good about himself or herself. This thing that can be done with the body and which feels so pleasurable is approved by her. The world is an unified whole. With tender hands, the mother caresses the baby. The cleaned and loved baby is put back comfortably into the crib. This baby learns a habit of relaxed, healthy acceptance of the self in the act of creation. Later, of course, when the baby gradually learns that he or she can make other things, this thing becomes of less importance. Mother and father, brother and sister, can make it too, and they put it in a special place. But this is later, much later.

Now see what happens if mother changes a diaper with disgust on her face and repulsion in her hands, as well as a "Messy baby!" in her voice. The baby holds its breath, its buttocks tighten, its little face screws up, and next time, instead of defecation being pure pleasure, it is marked by anxiety. Baby likes what h/she makes and the pleasure of making it, but mother doesn't like it. This is the essence of what the child learns.

Because the young baby cannot be easily successful in

the muscular control of a process for which there is not sufficient muscular maturity, the control, if it comes at all, is anxiety induced and creates nervous tension. This, in turn, truly interferes with the baby's physical and psychic health. It tends to make him or her more rigid, more compulsive, and leaves the child with less free energy for outgoing responses to people and situations. (Our adult misers of money and of love were once upon a time these babies whose toilet training was forced. Isn't it interesting that the very words we use to describe such persons are associated with the vernacular we use to express bowel movements, such as "He's loaded," or "He made a pile!"

Gradually, what is more important and more devastating to the baby, is the taking on of the mother's disgust for this whole part of the body, including the genitals. His or her anus begins to contract, not just when there is a need to defecate, but whenever a situation occurs in which he or she has to risk displeasure from mother. (Note how another conditioned reflex is built.) Later on, his or her anus contracts when there is a risk or displeasure from anyone at all, particularly authority figures. Don't many of us get "scared in the seat of our pants" when a traffic cop pulls up alongside us with a traffic violation?

Contrast this with the wisdom of Mother Nature, who has seen to it that there are pleasurable accompaniments to every natural process of the human body: eating, sleeping, breathing, eliminating, sexual functioning. When anxiety tensions and fear become associated with these processes, they are accompanied by pain and pathology. Colic, constipation, diarrhea, dysmenorrhea, painful intercourse are only a few of the end results of these earliest anxiety tensions.

On the other hand, the baby whose anus and genitals are accepted, who is approved as those developmental steps are taken that usher him or her from infancy toward adulthood, who is allowed to explore and to find genital pleasure, is the baby who is likely to grow into maturity with a minimum of sexual anxiety and a maximum of optimistic joy in outgoing responses to the man or woman who is his or her mate.

What is more, the good feelings about the self that result from approved and pleasurable bodily functions form the basis of *self-acceptance*. They are the roots of self-confidence, the biological sources from which a man or a woman knows himself or herself as worthy of love.

4

The Development of Lovingness—
Part Three: Givingness, Sharing Feelings, the Need for an Image of Love

Marriage (or any committed partnership of love) is a relationship that provides two people with the maximum opportunity for giving, one to the other. The capacity to give, however, begins in earliest infancy and must be nurtured. Its primary forms are not always recognized, and through lack of recognition and encouragement, the impulse to give withers and dies. Sometimes it seems to be almost deliberately stifled.

If, for example, a child brings his or her mother a wiggly worm or a dirty pebble (to the child a precious gift) and the mother makes the mistake of recoiling from the gift, this child's capacity to give is hurt. He or she becomes less sure of personal value and less spontaneous in sharing his or her enthusiasms.

On the other hand, if the mother can accept whatever the small boy or girl brings her, the child learns to enjoy sharing. Presently, as the child grows a bit older, tastes develop along more acceptably sophisticated lines and the observation of mother's needs begin. Then the child matches some of his or her gifts more appropriately with her desires. Most of all, confidence in capacity to please is developed. This is vitally important in marriage!

The earliest givingness, as we noted before, is the giving of excremental products, and babies tend to give these up more easily to relaxed and warmly accepting persons than to rigid, rejecting ones. A supervisor of a hospital nursery once told me that when a certain, stiff nurse came on duty, constipation afflicted the nursery, while other, warmer and more easy-going, nurses had all the diaper changing to do. This is confirmed by my observations of our own babies when they were held by occasional rigid visitors in our home. My husband and I soon learned not to expose our infants to the touch communication of such people.

Another early form of giving is the smile. Fortunately, babies have their smiles received and returned. Perhaps as a result, smiling is one of the least blocked of the human expressions of giving and response.

Less acceptable gifts, however, such as mud pies, clay baubles, messy paintings, etc., which reflect the child's attempts to make something pleasing, do not always meet with pleasure or acceptance on the part of the mother or father. Sometimes both the child and the gift are rejected and even repulsed, so that the child learns to distrust selected gifts and fears to give. Such a youngster develops little confidence creating and later seems to require that an authority figure put the stamp of approval or "correctness" upon it before he or she can "feel good" about what has been made. We see evidence of this all about us in human beings' need to be "correct." Some marital partners are, in fact, thrown into paroxysms of anxiety if their mate so much as wears something "different," or says something "out of line," or behaves "a bit daft" in the milieu of which he or she lives.

Originality and spontaneity in giving are delights in marriage. Part of my task, as I proceed, will be to indicate how such originality and spontaneity may be given rebirth in adult life.

Appreciation is another form of givingness that all of us need, yet, when its first crude beginnings are expressed by the child, we often fail to respond adequately.

This was first brought home to me by one of my college professors. I had been visiting in his home, wearing an outdated dress about which I was somewhat embarrassed. His small daughter, captivated by its color, said, "I like your pretty dress."

Uncomfortable with what I felt was this "undeserved" praise, I responded, "It's just an old one, and not very pretty, I'm afraid."

Overhearing her offering and my response, my professor gently took me by the arm and led me to the front porch, where we could talk privately.

"Do you know what you do to a child when you belittle or discredit her appreciation?" he asked. "A compliment is a gift, not to be thrown away carelessly unless you want to hurt the giver."

I hadn't thought of this before. But I did then, and have since. I also recalled that my own appreciative capacity, along with my ability to receive praise, was injured by adults who didn't believe that any one who complimented another could be "up to any good." This, by the way, I have found to be one of the most damaging false conclusions that a person can carry into a love relationship.

Responsiveness to the child leads to responsiveness on the part of the child. In adult love, a necessary ingredient is mutual responsiveness. All of us tend to pay more attention to the feelings of others when they have paid attention to ours—the process begins in childhood. Children whose parents have respected their sensitivity learn to trust themselves and to acknowledge other people's sensibilities. From there, they move on to discover ways to express feelings that are constructive and not destructive.

However, some adults tend to teach children to deny their perceptions of anger, jealously, loneliness, sorrow, pain, sex. These feelings are pushed underground, only to erupt at a later date in ways that are out of control and often destructive. When any slight stimulus in adult life triggers off this underground reserve of explosive emotion, the reactions produced may be quite out of keeping with the adult stimulus.

Another result of the denial of a child's honestly expressed feelings is suppression of emotion itself. In marriage, victims of this kind of conditioning cannot admit to their feelings, let alone expose them to their partners. Through lack of such exposure, they fail to have their real needs recognized or met. Then they tend to conclude falsely that no one really cares about them, least of all their wife—or husband.

An example or two of how this begins in childhood may prove fruitful when later we come to the task of re-educating ourselves for marriage.

Here is a common situation that occurs in many homes:

"I hate my little brother and I wish he were dead!" exclaims a three-year-old to her mother one day, when an eighteen-month-old baby brother has ruined her block building.

"Why, Mary!" reprimands mother, surprised and shocked by the child's virulence. "You know that you love your little brother. God doesn't like little girls who wish others dead."

This little girl now knows that her hostile feelings must be masked, for expression means rejection by mother. In

Givingness, Sharing Feelings, Need for Image of Love

addition, mother has invoked the image of God as a punishing Jehovah. Yet Mary's feelings are not dissipated. They are simply driven underground, and she now tries to hide them. Like all suppressed emotions, they gain in power and get out of control in sneaky ways. Later on, Mary, herself, becomes so disturbed by her own "unintentional" hostile behavior to her brother that she unconsciously terrorizes herself with nightmares in which she is "punished" by an avenging demon.

Suppose, instead, her mother had said, "Mary, I guess every boy and girl who ever lived has been annoyed by baby brothers and sisters. Babies can be an awful nuisance from time to time, however much we love them. I'm sorry he broke your building. Let mother help you build it up again and then we'll see if we can't keep Jimmy away from it."

Mary would have been comforted, her sense of injustice healed, and guilt about her temporary anger nonexistent. More important, having had her negative feelings accepted as valid, she would be more able to trust all her feelings and to communicate them. She would also be in a better position to control negative reactions by expressing them in some nondestructive way.

Other commonly heard denials of the feelings of children are all about us:

"I don't like Uncle Joe," says Sue.

"Yes, you do like your nice Uncle Joe. He is a good man," protests mother. Sue tries to force herself to like him, but loses, in the process, some trust in the validity of her own reactions to people. Later she may try to "make herself" love some "nice" man, completely uncertain as to what a love feeling really is.

"I hurted myself," cries Tommy, running to his mother.

"Big boys don't cry. It can't hurt that much," comments his mother. Tommy has learned that you cannot come to mother in tears without loss of "face." Later on, Tom, the man, cannot cry, even when he needs and wants to with the beloved of his life.

We could extend the list, but perhaps these examples are enough to show how we invalidate, by conditioning and repression, children's precious capacity to recognize and accept their own feelings and to deal with them honestly and constructively.

Every child needs an image of man-woman love lived out in the world about him. Such a vision provides him or her with knowledge "by osmosis," with absorption on the seeing-is-believing level. A child needs to feel the closeness of being cuddled between a mother and father who love each other and whose warm love radiations surround him or her, encompassing each other. This is warmth and protection in its most primitive sense. This is security deeply rooted. Such a child feels love and never doubts it.

What about the child growing up in a household, oh so civilized! where the husband and wife are outwardly garmented in the costumes of love, muttering time-honored lines of mother to father, but inwardly are cold as ice, and exploitative, bargaining, hard, and hateful. Where is this child to find the admirable images on which to fix his or her vision? Where are the warming radiations that should be absorbed?

Perhaps the presence of grandparents, aunts, or uncles, or even a neighboring couple into whose home the child is occasionally welcomed can save him or her but that child will have a tougher time when he or she comes to create a personal love relationship. Love may have to find its way to such a person through the rational processes of the "head" route, always more difficult and less secure. This represents a special problem that tenderness and wisdom can heal in adult life, but it may take time and patience.

The question, then, that faces all of us as we approach marriage, is this, "If our childhood experiences have incapacitated us so that it is difficult for us to move in a loving way, is there anything, as adults, that we can do about it? Can we be freed from our fears of feeling and of reaching? Can repressed anger, jealously, sadness, longing, be expressed so that others need not withdraw from us? Can we learn to reach so that others can respond to our needs?

In other words, can a person's love potential be re-established?

It is my experience that it can.

5
Filling Up the Cup

The conditions which we have noted as necessary for a child to grow into loving maturity become the essential clues to the continuing needs of the adult whom we hope to "fill up."

They are:

1. Responsiveness to "reach," particularly on the primary level of oral satisfaction and body contact.
2. Approval.
3. Acceptance of biological processes as good, particularly eating (including sucking), eliminating, genitality.
4. Acceptance of the expression and validity of feeling, positive and negative.
5. Acceptance of acts that represent givingness.
6. Availability of an image of love in the environment.

Because most of us have been somewhat injured we tend to behave like persons deeply afraid, even when our heads tell us that there is nothing to be afraid of. The result is that we often approach a loved being with a challenge instead of with an open expression of need. For example, a woman may say to her tired husband, "I don't suppose you'd like

Filling Up the Cup

to go to the movies with me tonight, would you?" the edge in her voice originating out of her own habitual negative expectations. His response, of course, is negative, and she feels "rejected" and "hurt." "He's always too tired to do anything with me" is the gist of her feeling.

Suppose, for a moment, that she had said "I'd love to see a movie tonight. Would you like to go after you've had a chance to eat and relax?" The chances are that he would have given himself time to become enthusiastic and that when he had rested he would have been delighted to accompany her. At the very least, he would have responded in a way that would have left her feeling loved and not rejected. For she, herself, has accepted her own desire as rational without acting as if those in her environment owed her satisfaction. If her husband could not meet her present need, she would feel neither deprived nor unloved. There would be other days and other times.

In the first instance, the woman has not accepted her right to want. She feels guilty and scared when she reaches. She waits till her desire for something is extreme before she can express it, and then her expression comes out hard, like a hammer blow, from which her lover can only withdraw. This leaves her more sure than ever that it doesn't pay to ask for what you want.

We *must* reach if we are going to find, yet we fear to reach because as infants we repeatedly met with frustration, pain, or punishment when we sought or found pleasurable fulfillment of some primary need. We became afraid to ask for anything personally satisfying to ourselves. After a bit, any deep desire tended to become tinged with anxiety lest a grim Fate snatch it from us. (How often do we "knock on wood," or indulge in ritualistic acts to protect our good luck!)

In reacquiring our capacity to reach, there is one very important point to keep in mind. A crucial and essential difference exists between the adult and the infant. As babies, we were truly helpless. When we "reached" fruitlessly there was little that we could do about it except rage or howl, which may have brought punishment and which, in turn, reinforced the false conclusion that "to reach brings pain." As adults, we are not helpless. By our own efforts we can obtain for ourselves the satisfaction of most of our primary needs, provided we are willing to pay the reasonable prices required by life.

Life's price, of course, is responsibility for our own acts, and immaturity lies in not recognizing this. Yet even the relatively mature person may have faulty notions as to what the price is for the fulfillment of a need, and these faulty notions can be very inhibiting and damaging.

For example, the man who assumes that the price of his wife's affection is a mink coat, when her real need is for his companionship, is the victim of a false emotional conclusion. He could not have made such an error had he not been conditioned to feel that he must bring a woman something that had monetary value in order to earn her love. Thus blinded, he cannot see or respond to his wife's real need.

There are three tasks we must perform in order to regain our capacity to "reach."

1. Dare to recognize what it is we really want.
2. Ask ourselves honestly what is its price, making sure that we have not drawn false emotional conclusions about the latter.
3. Be willing to accept a *yes* or *no* response (when we make "demands" instead of requests, they are, in essence, controlling. If a controlling relationship is maintained for very long, it spells the death of love)

It is surprising how hard it is for most people who are blocked in their "reach" to admit, even to themselves, what it is that they do want. They have defended themselves by wanting nothing or by accepting stereotypes

Filling Up the Cup

designed by society and wanting these stereotypes compulsively, without any real feeling of personal involvement or satisfaction, even when the wants are fulfilled.

In order to help people find out what their longings are, I use a technique which I have found very helpful. It often brings them into awareness of those emotional deprivations which form the basis of primary longings. It goes like this: I say, "Make a picture in your mind of the most important person in your life when you were little." (Usually it is mother or father, and most often, mother.) "Now, in your imagination, put that person in this room. Who is it?"

("Mother.")

"Do you see her?"

("Yes.")

"All right. What does she have on?"

("A yellow dress with blue flowers on the collar.")

"Fine. Now *you* make this mother sit down over here on the couch. Can you see her?"

("Yes.")

"Is she sitting where you want her?"

("Yes.")

"Now, *you* make her do something that would be a pleasure to you."

Usually this brings a return question such as "Do you mean a pleasure to me right now, or a pleasure in the past, when I was a child?"

I answer, "A pleasure to you at any time. It doesn't matter. But make her do something that would please you. And when you see it happening, tell me about it."

There is usually a pause; then sometimes a smile, often followed by tears, if not sobs. I acknowledge these, but press on, again and again and again instructing, "Now make her do something else that would be a pleasure to you."

Little by little by little the person seeking help begins to acknowledge longing for the satisfaction of deep childhood needs, usually compounded of those elements we noted in our list of conditions under which any child develops lovingness: things like being held, caressed, fed, paid attention to, received with pleasure. Or like having mother accept a gift of a dirty pebble or a frog, with all the delight with which it was given. Or like having mother trust and give ever increasing freedom to find one's own way. Or like having mother love father with open affection and treating him with respect. These and many more.

More often than not, an hour of such a procedure releases the flood gate that has been shut against desire. And it almost invariably shows the individual what he or she must have the courage to reach for and to accept in order to fill the vacuums created by deprivation in his or her infancy, childhood, and youth. It is only as these vacuums are filled that our adult can move along into mature expressions of loving.

He or she may even learn that sometimes the full "price" of satisfying a longing is daring to reach for its gratification in a tender way, daring to say to someone loved that there are needs of this kind; and daring to let the beloved satisfy them in the present. I have known many a man and a woman to fill up their hungers by such simple deeds as bathing each other, feeding each other, a woman offering her breast to her husband (not as to a lover, now, but as to a tiny, starved infant who needs to receive warmth and succor from a mother); a husband holding his wife in his lap as a father might hold his little girl, maybe even offering her something to suck, like his thumb, perhaps. Through these, and other experiences like them, lovers may live out their repressed longings and heal injured areas which, through the pain of deprivation, have kept them from "growing up."

Sometimes people ask if such "indulgences" won't prolong and encourage infantilism. Actually, the reverse is the

Filling Up the Cup

case. In an unbelievably short time, the sense of deprivation is dissipated and the individual feels able to move away from childhood hungers because they have at long last, been filled. It *is* possible to feel very anxious when one first permits oneself such primary gratification. This is due to a "triggering off" of fear memories of the-baby-of-long-ago who had to face frustration when he or she reached for fulfillment. This time give him or her approval and satisfaction and watch the anxiety recede.

Recently, I had reported to me one of the most touching instances of such healing that I have ever encountered. It made me glad that I could be the catalyst for its occurrence.

An intelligent and charming young couple had come to me for marriage counseling. In the course of our sessions, the girl bride complained of her own lack of contact with people and her sense of being perpetually disapproved of in social situations. This sometimes included even her husband. Shortly thereafter, she reported a series of recurring dreams that seemed to me reminiscent of the experience of birth.

They were particularly vivid sensory images of passing through a dark tunnel from which she emerged into the presence of a strange yellow light that resembled the amber of a particular kind of electric bulb. The walls of the chamber were gleaming white like those of a tiled operating room. She was placed in a transparent coffin through which the light penetrated constantly. She saw disapproving faces of people hovering over the enclosure, then going away from her. Always they left, and always she could not touch them. Upon awakening, she invariably experienced a terrifying desolation.

I asked her what she knew about her own birth. Puzzled by my question, she told me that she had been a premature baby, having spent the first six weeks of her life in an incubator.

"Would life in an incubator resemble your perception of yourself in your dream?" I asked.

A light, like dawn, broke over her face, as she played with the idea, sampling its application to her present reactions to adult social situations. She noted that she had perceived herself as disapproved and without contact. This conformed to her actual initial experience of life, either as she actually experienced it or as she later heard about it and relived it in fantasy. Had these earliest weeks provided her with false, outdated, emotional conclusions about herself? Might experiences which she could not consciously remember have conditioned her to a self-conception that needed reconditioning to heal?

Some curious physical yearnings emerged for her about this time. She had been conscious of them before but had pushed them out of her mind. Now they seemed to confirm the notion of "unfinished business" surrounding her birth. She yearned to reenact the drama and this time to be held closely and warmly next to a human body.

These longings were communicated to her husband, along with the story of her dream.

One night, about a week later, when they lay curled in each other's arms, she felt an indescribable impulse to act out this experience, shaping it now on her own terms. Wordlessly her husband watched and waited, cooperating as well as he could. She crawled under the blankets and pushed her head against his legs. When she had burrowed enough, she allowed herself to be "born." Then she wanted to be picked up and caressed.

At this point, her husband, inadequately informed of her desire and intent, failed his cue and the girl burst into sobbing out of all proportion to the occasion. As he held her trembling body, she tried to tell him of her curious and almost insatiable longing to be gathered up and held immediately after a "birth" experience. Wisely, he urged her

Filling Up the Cup

to try the drama again, letting him participate with more sensitivity and awareness. She agreed. This time, he played his role of deliverer and welcomer to its fullest and warmest, snuggling his wife in a plethora of kisses and caresses that seemed to bring her into contactful relationship with her surroundings. She experienced this "rebirth" as a healing process of the greatest magnitude.

This couple had been able, through love, to do for each other what few therapists in the world could do, namely, set up new conditioning, through positive action. The healing of love had made it more possible for the wife to feel acceptable and to be in greater contact with her environment.

This story brings me to the statement of a principle which I consider crucial in the healing of emotional wounds and which has hardly begun to be recognized, let alone be acted upon.

The principle is based on the knowledge that much, if not most, of the serious damage done to people has occurred in the first two years of their lives on the preverbal level of development. Just talking about these things rarely seems to result in healing. The original communication received by the individual was a touch, sight, smell conditioning that physically influenced self-perception. In my experience, the healing process begins when new conditioning is experienced, which approximates fulfillment of the need felt by the infant of long ago, changing his or her *adult* self-perception and correcting emotional conclusions.

As I have pointed out, these needs are likely to be in one or more of the following areas: sucking; being held; affirmation by approving touch of the whole body, particularly of the mouth, the genitals, and the buttocks; affirmation of the individual's right to enjoy his or her own genitals; permissive allowance of anger and tears; and responsiveness to "reach."

Marriage counselors have an unprecedented opportunity to make use of this principle by indicating to marital partners various ways that they can help to bring healing to each other. With a little informed questioning and some observations based on extensive clinical experience, a marriage counselor can help two persons to find where the hurt and unfulfilled areas are, indicating to each what the other's needs are, trusting that their love will find creative ways to carry them through their experiment. Again and again it works. People convinced that their persons and their natural functions are ugly and "no good" begin to feel lovable and loved when their mates caresses into life a heretofore rejected body or rejected function. A man and wife can provide the touch approval of the mouth, the buttock, the genitals that was denied to the baby.

One simple act of fulfillment that women have known since the Garden of Eden is the offering of food to the beloved at the moment of depleted energy or of emotional need. This reminds me of a witty comment made by the lovable Abraham Stone, to the effect that "The trouble with the Garden of Eden was not that there was a red apple in it, but that there was a green pair."

Eve was *not* green about offering food. However, modern Eves may need to be reminded that it is a primary act of love to offer food when their man needs it, without waiting for civilized rituals, like mealtime, etc.

The Japanese girl is said to be waiting at the door of her home, immediately ready to offer two gifts of love to her homecoming mate; caressing hands that know how to massage away the abrasive effects of his skirmishes with the workaday world, and tea or saki for the immediate refreshment of his body. Both gifts are deeply reminiscent of maternal acts that shape the baby's perception of the world as good, as giving. Both men and women who face the workaday world need the equivalent of these Japanese girls.

A young husband I know had been distressed by his wife's lack of hand dexterity. He considered her ineptitude and inefficiency a liability, although he tried his hardest to give her the encouragement which he sensed she needed. However, her awkward and time-consuming struggles with simple household chores sometimes drove him to a distraction which he could not conceal.

One relaxed evening, as they both sat by the fire reading, he glanced up and noticed that she was picking her fingers, almost to the quick.

"What can I do to keep that from happening?" he asked, with gentle concern.

"Love my hands!" came her answer, so spontaneously that even she was startled by it.

Acting upon this insight, he laid her hands against his face and, placing one of her fingers after another inside his mouth, he kissed and caressed them with his tongue, and held each warmly inside his cheek.

While her tears boiled over as she felt the impact of his love streaming into her hands, she began to understand how she had detested them, associating them with her mother's negative criticism of her. ("You're so awkward; you're a bull in a china shop.") This moment with her husband was like a freeing key unlocking a door.

Whether this simple act of love will help to heal her hand clumsiness is yet to be seen, but my hunch is that it will free her from some of her anxiety tensions so that, in time, her hands, with their new feeling of "being loved" will develop normal skills. Whether or not this happens, however, the tender gratitude evoked by his recognition of her need sings out as a soul-healing moment between them.

6
Dissolving the Blocks to Lovingness

A principle that is worth understanding, at least in its simplest terms, is that any emotion which is repressed is accompanied by body tensions, for emotion is feeling that wants to move out, wants expression. When a strong feeling, like anger, is held in, therefore, it is controlled muscularly, as well as in one's mind. The result is muscular stiffness through which no soft, tender feeling can find expression until the body tensions of anger are dissolved. (Anger, please note, need not be against the beloved. It may be a cumulative, hateful feeling carried since childhood and set off by some recent event, such as a dressing down by the boss.) People, from time immemorial, have appreciated the need (and the wisdom) of exorcising (getting rid of) such muscular tensions and have, consciously or unconsciously, done so through aggressive activities like chopping wood, playing golf, scrubbing kitchen floors, banging doors, crashing dishes, etc.

I teach young couples, most of whom live in city apartments and can't bang doors or chop wood, the therapeutic value of standing on their own two feet and whamming a

Dissolving the Blocks to Lovingness

couch with both fists; or of lying on their backs with their legs in the air and crashing them down hard on a bed; or of scratching their fingers across a firm surface, like a cat at a tree stump; or of strangling a pillow with their hands.

At first they think that this is foolish nonsense, and they approach it with great timidity and embarrassment. Once they have tried it, however, at the moment when anger tensions are mounting toward the explosion point, they comment, "What a surprise! I don't feel tied up in knots any more."

One of my patients, the father of two obstreperous boys, rigged up a canvas duffel bag, stuffed his wife's old cleaning rags in it, and swung it by a sturdy rope from a beam in the doorway between the lads' rooms. It became the recipient of kicks, punches, tackles, and ferocious onslaughts, not only of the boys, but of all the members of this family. The husband reports that everyone, including the family dog, has benefited. His wife admits that even *she* gives it an occasional kick on her way to answer the invasive telephone.

Another patient invested in an assortment of sponges, upon which he drains off his biting angers. He tells me that he rips into these sponges with tooth and jaw, spitting their pieces half across the room, and then feels as docile as a lamb. His wife occasionally grapples with an old pillow which she strangles with zest. Then they both feel good and usually end up making love.

Most women, and a good many men, are terribly afraid of primitive physical expressions of anger. On occasion, when I have suggested that a real explosion might make a person feel better, the usual response is "Something terrible might happen," or "If I really let go, I might take a wall down." Some women will start to cry if I so much as propose that they give themselves a chance to explode in any way except verbally.

Once a young cop showed me his scarred right hand, mute testimony to a past fury that had "gotten out of control." It was a gnarled club, with a great healed gash running from forefinger to wrist. "Once I got so mad at the sergeant that I put my fist right through the door," he told me. "Since then, I just clench my fingers and hang on hard. Seems as though I'm angry most of the time, come to think of it, and now my wife complains that I don't know how to touch her gently. So I've ended up not touching her at all. She doesn't like that either; and neither do I."

I suggested that he might "let go" on the firm mattress in my office. He looked incredulous, but took up the challenge. His incredulity before the attack was as nothing to what it was afterward. "Well! I'll be damned!" he exulted, a new glint in his eye. "That works, doesn't it!" as he looked at his relaxed hands. "Do you think my wife will feel their difference?"

I assured him that I thought she would, and I wasn't wrong.

The penalties for anger have been so severe at early ages that it never seems to dawn on anyone that there needn't *be* a penalty or that there is nothing intrinsically wrong with expressing anger if there are no casualties. The trick is to give vent to primary physical activity that correctly reflects the primary physical desire, such as punching, kicking, biting, screaming, etc., but to do so in such a way that no one gets hurt and nothing of value gets broken. This includes exploding the howls and yowls, cussings and cursings that may also have been denied expression. Some people I know drive out in the country where they can "blow off steam" by screaming.

If you think this is silly, try it some time, observing your own feelings before and after. If you can remove fear and casualty from anger, you will have found a therapeutic tool of the greatest importance to your marriage. If you find

Dissolving the Blocks to Lovingness

yourself getting frightened of the expression of anger, remember that repression is not the same thing as control. Control of any emotion is achieved only when one knows how to use it for one's own good and without harm to anyone else. This kind of control always leads to a more free-flowing friendliness in a human relationship. Repression, on the other hand, which is so often mistaken for self-control, is likely to behave destructively, leading to the freezing up of love feelings.

Another kind of armoring comes with the holding in of tears. A man may need to cry, or even to sob, but he is afraid of being a baby. He has been so fear-frozen in childhood about the unmanliness of crying that he suffers needless agonies in maintaining a defensive stoicism in adulthood. Men learn too well to "keep a stiff upper lip," to put "starch in their spines," to project their jaws, and to "swallow down" their sobs.

But, as in the repression of anger, when so much muscular effort goes into the prevention of the flow of tears, one cannot experience a flow of love, for love cannot move through a muscular blockade. Tears have, as their healthy function, the healing release of sorrow. They should be welcomed.

A wife may need all the skill she can develop to encourage her husband to cry when he needs to.

One wife I know discovered that if she caressed her husband's neck and throat when she saw him swallowing down a sob and said something like this to him, "Don't swallow down your feelings. Please give them up to me. You can trust me with them," he then could relax his throat and cry.

Another woman, when she observed her husband's spine start to stiffen, knew that this was his way of bracing himself against a sob. He was a social worker whose profession confronted him with a great deal of tragedy about which he often felt helpless. It is worth noting that he also suffered excruciating backaches at these times. His wife learned that if she affirmed his right to feel sad, and then put her arms around his waist, massaging his back and laying his head onto her breast, that eventually he could give way and let the wracking sobs burst forth. When finished, his backache would be gone and his burden of sadness laid aside, leaving him able to face the next day's assignment with zest and optimism.

Release of primary feeling is always experienced as "good." Body tensions disappear, including the physical distress signals which invariably accompany repressed emotion, such as the backache of this man, or the stomach-ache of another. Pain, please note, is a valuable clue to frozen feeling. Wise physicians have known for a long time that there is a direct relationship between many illnesses suffered by their patients and their psychic burdens. Some have dared to act upon this knowledge, with impressive results.

A masseuse I know runs her experienced fingers over the skin surfaces of her clients, correctly locating the place or places where there is a muscular spasm, or knot of tension (which is usually experienced as painful to touch), and then she gently but firmly massages these places, instructing her client to breath out as she does so. The relief from pain is almost instantaneous, sometimes coming so dramatically that the individual experiences it as a "miracle." Headaches may disappear within seconds, contracted throats may expand into speech, and griping stomach cramps may relax, to mention only a few examples of tension that may be eased.

In identifying emotionally induced pain, a useful rule of thumb for the untrained person is to ask oneself what kinds of experiences precede one's most frequent illness, for example, one's colds, one's headaches, one's bouts of

Dissolving the Blocks to Lovingness

diarrhea, one's "accidents." What associations are set off as one dares to challenge oneself with the question: "Why did I need this illness?" or "What results did I achieve by this accident?" or "What body tensions did I feel most persistently just prior to the onset of distress?"

It has been my experience that one can often bypass an illness by alertness to tension together with its immediate dissipation through direct action therapy.

Another way people block their feelings is by holding their breath or breathing in a shallow, barely perceptible manner, with chest held high and pelvis retracted. We must release this block to feeling whenever we wish to give expression to love. As I noted in an earlier chapter, anxiety or fear is the primary reason for such breathing. However, it becomes chronic so early in life that many people are hardly aware that their breathing is like this most of the time.

A deliberate release of the breath in full exhalation helps to dissipate anxiety. In other words, you can consciously and purposefully lessen fear by learning how to breathe. In addition, you can greatly increase pleasurable sexual feeling; but a discussion of the latter I will leave to another chapter where I intend to go into the subject in some detail.

Public speakers and actors know this remedy for stage fright and practice it assiduously. Mothers who are training themselves for natural childbirth learn this method of breathing. It performs for them, among other things, the very important function of freeing them from fear-induced tensions during the process of labor. This, in turn, reduces pain that is caused by tension, which is the most usual source of pain in childbirth.

Dozens of times in every day the average man or woman finds use for the technique of complete exhalation. Yet it is surprising how difficult it is to persuade people to acquire sufficient skill so that it becomes second nature. (I really should have said "first nature," for this is the kind of breathing we were born with before the scare-aches of our environment were built into us.)

To reacquire such breathing skill, lie flat on your back, with a small pillow under your knees. Let all the air out of your lungs, permitting your chest to curve slightly toward your knees in a gentle arc during the exhalation. If you are doing it correctly, you will feel a streaming, pleasurable sensation traveling down through your abdomen and into your legs.

The most frequent problem encountered by anxious people when they are first relearning to breathe is that the exhalation gets stuck at the diaphragm because the latter is contracted. In fact, the common complaint of the anxious person is "I can never draw an easy breath." A simple way to release the diaphragmatic block is to stick your finger down your throat, eliciting a gag reflex, which will break the contraction.

If the block does not readily yield in this manner, lie on your stomach and get your husband (or wife) to run his (her) hands down your back until the muscular tensions are located. These can be recognized by your reaction to sensitivity to touch. Massage these "knots" until they dissolve. At first, the firm, circular movement of the massaging hand hurts. When this occurs, breathe out and also permit the expression of any sound or expletive that you feel like. (It could be a shout, a sob, or a cuss word—never mind what.) These sounds are sometimes quite surprising, occasionally even shocking to the uninitiated.

Gradually, as the tension lessens, so does the pain and presently you feel "completely relaxed" and able to surrender yourself to the ebb and flow of pleasurable feelings. Also, your breathing is no longer blocked at the diaphragm. Again and again partners exclaim, "Why, this is a miracle!"

Dissolving the Blocks to Lovingness

I assure them that it is no miracle, but rather the result of a technique that any couple can learn and administer to each other with benefit to both.

Although this process is absurdly simple, it is surprising how difficult it is for anyone who is rigidly "bound up" to "let go" and relax without some such help and specific training. If you live in a city where there is a bioenergetically trained therapist who is acquainted with techniques of release of neuromuscular "blocks" of emotional origin, it is very helpful to get him or her to instruct you. However, even if you have no resource available to you, you can still experiment considerably on your own with great benefit to you and your mate.

The man or woman who wishes to help a partner dissolve blocks to loving expression must also learn to *receive* the negative feelings of that mate, knowing that when these are accepted, he, or she, can deal with the problems behind the feelings more rationally and honestly. This is usually done by a quiet acknowledgment of what the other is experiencing without any attempt to defend, contradict, or refute. Irrational as they may seem to the onlooker, feelings are always valid to the person who experiences them. What may be "invalid," is the set of false assumptions on which they may be based and at a *later* time these need to be attacked vigorously. At the moment, however, the most helpful and comforting reaction is simply to listen receptively.

One can rout out one's own false emotional conclusions by the practice of what I call "the daily review." Many people consider it too much of a chore, but those who have tried it discover enriching insights and a blessed lessening of those destructive feelings which are based on incorrect assumptions. It consists in jotting down on paper the details of any incident during the day when an unpleasurable tension has been experienced. The pattern of cause and effect will not be apparent until the process has been carried out for a week or two, perhaps longer. The triggering-off incidents will vary, but the theme will emerge strong and clear, usually yielding a series of attitudes based on invalid assumptions. The following are typical: "My husband didn't remember my birthday; therefore he doesn't love me." "She doesn't iron my shirts the way my mother ironed them; ergo, she isn't an efficient housekeeper." "If my husband doesn't agree with the boss, he must be wrong and will soon lose his job."

Potentially, such wrong assumptions may be very dangerous and destructive to a marriage. For quite clearly, if your attitude toward your mate is based on a faulty emotional conclusion, you are likely to react in negative and defensive ways. If you want a marital relationship that is relatively free of resentment, it is always necessary to take responsibility for correcting your own false assumptions or to seek help in doing so.

Sometimes expressions of love feelings are clogged by unexpressed complaints. A simple expedient for the removal of such a block may be through a process we call "catharsis"; in other words, the dumping of one's complaints into the listening ear of another person. This is a job that marriage counselors are especially trained for. In fact, I often jokingly describe myself as the "complaint department." Chips on the shoulder, injured feelings, real or fancied thoughtlessness from the beloved, etc. can choke off the flow of love if they are not disposed of. When these are thoroughly exorcised, one feels washed clean.

There is a rule to follow in this kind of cleansing, however. *Negative* criticism directed to one's mate is worse than a body blow, and in many ways is more destructive. Few people can stand very much of it and still remain lovers. So, just as you get rid of anger by hitting a punching bag, not your wife, so you exorcise your feelings

Dissolving the Blocks to Lovingness

about real or imagined insults and injuries by hurtling them at a marriage counselor; or by writing them down on a piece of paper and consigning it to the fire; or by shouting expletives into the wind on a solitary walk. It helps to have one's complaints heard by a trusted confidante who will listen uncritically and then forget what he has heard. When your anger has drained off, and along with it the irrational, pain-giving elements of your dissatisfaction, you may be in a position to state your criticism in *positive* terms directly to your mate. It has a chance then to function effectively, to produce desired action, to be heard receptively.

Incidentally, when you are faced with behavior in another that you do not like, a useful procedure is to ask, "What might have happened to make the other person behave like that? Why is he or she that way?" If you do this conscientiously, you will find that so many hurtful influences have been at work that you wil begin to wonder why the situation wasn't worse. Then you will marvel at the enormous reaching for goodness there is in all people which makes them as wonderful as they are. When such a feeling begins to take over, you will find yourself becoming appreciative instead of critical. Then comes what often seems like a miracle: as you give free rein to the expression of appreciation, you find real growth changes in the persons you love. These occur, impressively, along the lines of your expressed approval.

However, mutual appreciation is, itself, sometimes severely blocked. We have already noted how this blockade was built up in childhood. To dissolve it and thus set in motion the healing effect of appreciation, I often ask my marriage counseling couples a question such as the following:

"Tell me, John, what are some of the things that made you fall in love with Mary?"

Mary, of course, is standing by, with hungry ears.

Then I reverse the question "And Mary, what made you fall in love with John? What did you like about him?"

Sometimes this can be phrased another way, which tends to bring to each an increased knowledge of the needs of the other. I ask, "What could Mary do to please you, John?" And vice versa.

Sometimes I enlist their cooperation in trying a game that goes like this:

"Mary, think of a compliment for John and tell it to him here. John, when you hear the compliment, accept it as a gift, making Mary glad, by your response, that she has made you this present."

Back and forth they toss and catch and toss again the ball of praise until each has gotten over the embarrassment and frozenness about giving and receiving compliments.

So many times a woman says that she wishes to hear her husband say, "I love you," yet he will demur with, "The words stick in my throat. I just can't make my mouth say them."

This, of course, is a block, for he loves her but his expression of it needs thawing. Sometimes the love words won't come out because there is such a clutter of angry words that have not been said (having been repressed because they couldn't be said to authority figures in childhood. Primarily, it isn't to his wife that his anger is directed). It may also be that his love expressions were rejected in childhood and finally froze into an "I won't love." Now there is an "I can't" whenever he wants to express love to his wife.

His wife must begin by receiving graciously whatever act of his may be considered a gift, remembering that this is the way a person gains confidence in the giving of gifts of emotional value. If she can acknowledge verbally to her husband, for example, that his going out to work and bringing home the rewards of that work are, in her eyes,

Dissolving the Blocks to Lovingness

tremendously important gestures of love, she is helping to break down his resistance to telling her that he loves her. Likewise, the husband who tells his wife that he understands and appreciates her contributions is also making a gift that dissolves her resistance to more direct verbal appreciation of him. Any appreciative gesture opens up the heart responses which we know as affection. They "touch" us and help us to lower our defenses, to move trustingly in more feelingful ways.

7
Communication in Marriage

"Let the spirit in you move your lips and direct your tongue. Let the voice within your voice speak to the ear within (your friend's) ear; for his soul will keep the truth of your heart as the taste of the wine is remembered when the color is forgotten and the vessel is no more."*

Communication is the art of sharing experience. When we commune deeply with another, we enter into another's life, and that person enters into ours. We have a sense of greater completion, of unification, and of well-being.

However, because of many factors operating in our cultural milieu, indeed, in the "civilized" world at large, we may tend to become rigid and separated, rather than fluid and unified. The more this occurs, the more miserable we feel.

One reason that falling in love is so enjoyable is that, for the time being, at least, we feel able to melt our differences in oneness, build a bridge across our separateness, identify without becoming identical; in other words, we feel com-

---

*Kahlil Gibran, *The Prophet*. Published by Alfred A. Knopf, Inc., New York, N.Y.

pleted. The high tide of new love washes over us, temporarily carrying off our fears, which permits us to offer our thoughts and feelings, dreams and aspirations to the tender reception of the beloved.

But we are not very experienced in such sharing. Some of us are so frightened by self-exposure that the slightest unexpected movement sends us running to cover. There we stand, shivering and alone, in our little hiding places, till we can bear the loneliness no longer and then we cry out for help.

Indeed, there is no pain quite so agonizing as that of being out of communication. We speak of the truly bereft person as one who is "out of touch," is "contactless." If you ask any of your friends what could make them wish to die, most would tell you, "Being shut away from all other people." The isolation cell is not an accidental cruelty. History is full of tales of ingenious persons who used their inner resources to invent ways to keep their minds intact under such circumstances.

Most of us, of course, don't have to face anything so punishing, yet we find ourselves in a kind of cage with the door latched from the inside, complaining that we feel locked away from human fellowship, particularly from our mate.

What we are saying is that we don't know how to get outside our own shells, or we don't dare. After the first flush of loving communication in marriage, and the first scared flight away from it, we meet our mate on the barren land of safe "substitutes" for communion. We talk about the weather, about the activities of the children and the neighbors, encompassing the "price of everything and the value of nothing." Presently we become bored with this monotony and yearn for what we imagine is the free and adventurous land beyond the cage. Some couples think that dissolution of the marriage will solve their problem, but others, with greater insight, realize that they must learn the art of communication: what it is, how it works, how it can be deepened and made relatively safe yet adventurous. They intend to experience their marriage in richer terms.

Such couples may seek out a marriage counselor.

Just as travelers going to foreign lands need guides to teach them the language of the country, so do men and women entering marriage need skilled counselors to help them understand and sensitively use our many ways of interpersonal communication. They want to know why we open up with one person and close up with another, expand at one time and contract at another. They want to know what can be done to promote a healthy interchange of thought and feeling and why the road to such interchange is so often blocked.

This is what I, as a marriage counselor, might tell these couples. Communication is of two kinds, verbal and non-verbal. Both are important avenues to a full sharing of life with those whom we love.

The wiser we become, however, the more we pay attention to what people say without words; say with their eyes, their muscles, their body odors, their skin temperatures, their habitual ways of moving, the tones of their voices. We depend on and react to these communication unconsciously, and, indeed, they are more dependable than the spoken word. Until we have developed some conscious awareness of the messages they carry, we have hardly understood living life at all, let alone the nuances of perception required in marriage.

This should not surprise anybody. In mankind's evolution, language was very late in arriving on the scene, but expressive movements have been with us since the beginning of man's life on earth and are the very core of our beings. They are "built in," so to speak. They carry our message more completely, more honestly than any words we may superimpose upon them. The latter we don, like fancy dress for a ball, for much of the verbiage of adult life is a mask of meaning.

A child learns early in life that with honest self-expression the result may sometimes be too painful to bear. But he or she also learns that one will be held responsible only for spoken thoughts. So his or her words say one thing, and nonverbal expressiveness may say something quite different. In the latter, one may love or hate, caress or kill, build up or destroy with apparent impunity. Nevertheless, ones unspoken communications are received as surely as they are sent, even if they seem unacknowledged. Both sender and receiver react emotionally to their impact even while relegating the message to the unconscious.

Note a few examples of this potent language; you will be able to find countless others as you permit yourself some awareness of your own body reactions.

We might begin by observing how various forms of expressive movement have cropped up in the speech patterns we use to describe our impressions of other people. Pay attention to these.

We say, "A man has a chip on his shoulder" when, in truth, his shoulders are hunched up in resentful holding-in of anger.

We say, "She is stiff-necked" (unbending or unyielding); or "She grinds her teeth" (is furious); or "She is a cold fish" (has no warm body radiations); and so on.

We draw in our breath in anxiety (tension); we let it go out in pleasure (relaxation). In anxiety, our breathing is thoracic, shallow, barely perceptible, and our chest is held high. With release of the anxiety we exhale (the degree of the exhalation being a measure of the degree of the release).

In pleasure, we are aware of the "streamings" that accompany expiration and which, as I mentioned earlier, travel down over the abdomen through the pelvis and into our extremities, bringing warmth and glow to all skin surfaces.

The held-in breath, the high, tight chest, the stiff stomach, the jutting jaw, the pursed lips, the squared shoulders perched atop a ramrod spine, the retracted pelvis, the cold eyes and clenched fists speak to us of defensiveness, of rigidity, of armoring, particularly against tenderness, or pleasure, or receptivity. We would not consider disclosing our deep and tender dreams or exposing our embryonic thoughts to a person so defended. Nor would we bring our wounds to him or her for healing.

On the other hand, when we see a person whose breath is exhaling freely from a relaxed and moving chest, with soft lips in a mobile mouth, with warm, caressing eyes, and sloping shoulders above a flexible back, a tension-free stomach, pelvis curving slightly forward, and warm hands, we feel quite differently. Here we know that we could talk and be heard by such a person, love and be loved, expose wounds and have them cared for tenderly.

What about the tone of voice as a form of nonverbal communication? (Sounds preceded speech by millions of years.) For example, we know by their sounds whether children playing in the next room are at peace or if war is likely to break out momentarily. We "hear" panic, or excitement, or sorrow, or joy, or anger, from afar. We hear by tone, before words are distinguished.

Listen to some of the descriptive words we use to communicate the emotional effect upon us of tone: "harsh," "rasping," "purring," "soothing," "imperious," "coaxing," "murderous," "seductive," "loving," to mention only a few.

The tone our words are spoken in denotes the difference between love and hate, warmth and coldness, acceptance and rejection. One person can actually say, "I hate you," and make it sound like impassioned love. Another may say,

"I love you," and make you feel as if you had been stabbed in the back on a dark night.

Next to expressive movements, touch is the most primitive of our communication systems.

There are persons who can touch a skittery horse, and the beast calms instantly. There are physicians who can lay their hands on a sick person, and the patient visibly shows that he or she feels the promise of healing. There are lovers whose caressing fingers can melt the resistance of any person not carved of stone.

But there are also those from whose touch we recoil as surely as if we had been stung by a venomous snake. The hand that wants to slap, or punch, or scratch is not going to carry the same message as the hand that wants to caress or heal.

In my office, I have seen a man's hands clench while the words his mouth frames are "Of course, I love my wife. She is a good woman, but—."

"But what are your hands saying?"

More than likely his answer is, "They'd like to wring her neck."

When I toss him a pillow, the strangling he gives it leaves no doubt of the fury that he was holding back in his clenched fists.

If the hand that wants to wring a neck (not necessarily the beloved's, by the way) tries to caress hers at the same time, it may get across a confused message, at best; and at worst, a result comparable to that of the character in Steinbeck's novel "Of Mice and Men" (who murdered his beloved mouse while petting it and later, did the same thing to his girl).

Incidentally, when we feel a need to strangle, claw, punch, kick, bite, and scream (and show me the person so serene that such feelings are not experienced from time to time) we should give ourselves a chance to get the wringing, the clawing, scratching, punching, kicking, biting, and screaming out on inanimate objects before approaching any creature toward whom we wish to express affection or love. Otherwise, the touch communication is destructive.

Odor is another nonverbal language.

Most body exudation, including breath, have good smells when the human being is "feeling good."

The smell of love, particularly, is so alluring that the poets of all time have tried to express its delights in words. Listen to the Song of Solomon, that beautiful antiphonal poem where man and maid each try to outdo the other in verbal caresses:

Because of the savor of thy good ointments thy name is as ointment poured forth, therefore do the virgins love thee.

A bundle of myrrh is my well beloved unto me; he shall lie all night betwixt my breasts.

My beloved is unto me as a cluster of camphire.

How fair is thy love, my sister, my spouse! how much better is thy love than wine! and the smell of thine ointments than all spices!

Now also thy breasts shall be as clusters of the vine, and the smell of thy nose like apples.

Little animals, human and otherwise, have warmed themselves by the breath of maternal love. Most mother creatures know, by the smell of their babies, especially by their bowel movements, the state of their children's health.

On the other hand, when the human being is suffering anxiety or nursing hate, his exudations create an unpleasing odor. The dragon of mythology, emitting sulphurous fumes, makes me believe that human kind has, for a long time, recognized bad smell as a communication of frustrated, hateful fury.

Communication in Marriage

If you really want to understand another person, imitate his or her expressive movements. (Children do this intuitively, by the way. It is one reason they leap language barriers so easily.) Find, in your own musculature, what is being enacted in another's, and presently his or her feelings will become startlingly clear to you.

What you do with these true messages is another story.

At first, you can simply acknowledge them to yourself, letting them percolate through to the level of your own conscious awareness. Later, as you learn to trust the accuracy of your perceptions and the authenticity of nonverbal communications, you will want to gauge your actions by the true messages you hear and not be misguided by spoken ones that often mask rather than reveal. As you learn to make your responses reflect your understanding of the unspoken, as well as the spoken, you will achieve a deeper and more mature communication with your loved one. I might add that you will also encourage more verbal honesty if you are able to refrain from judgmental or critical reactions to these revelations.

For example, a sexually frightened wife says to her husband every night at bedtime, "I have a headache." Obviously, he hasn't recognized the thousand and one signals her body has already given him that should have alerted him to her real need and her real problem. When he can accept and act upon what she is really saying, she can find the courage to say, "I'm afraid of sex because I never really have any pleasure from it. Help me find my pleasure."

Or a tired husband, contemplating his lawn on a Sunday morning, doesn't have to develop an upset stomach if his wife can take in the situation and say "You've worked hard all week. You really need this day for rest and relaxation. Let's see that you get it."

This leads me to say again that we should pay attention to our own body reactions. Often we are deaf, dumb, and blind to our own true feelings, like persons cut off from vital parts of themselves. Certainly we can never establish communication with another human being until we have established it with ourselves, including the significance of our somatic symptoms.

Not only in nonverbal language but in speech itself we have much to learn about communication. We soon discover that there are discrepancies between what *we* mean by the words we say and the impact of these words upon those we love. Words may have emotional meanings to one person that are not shared by another, some being so emotionally "charged" that their use sets off surprising reactions. Sometimes they seem to place one at opposite poles from the beloved. To cope with this dilemma, we must recognize that any word is learned, conditioned by one's environment. It is a symbol attached to experience. If the associative experience is painful, the use of the word by another may trigger off pain-giving reactions.

Pavlov, the Russian scientist, experimented with conditioned reflexes. One of his experiments consisted of feeding a dog some meat and simultaneously ringing a bell. Presently, the dog became so "conditioned" to the presence of meat when a bell rang that the sound itself became the stimulus for salivation, even when no meat accompanied it. (Remember that salivation is a somatic response, generally not under conscious control.) Everyone of us is like Pavlov's dog in some respects. We are conditioned to react to words in certain ways, often with no conscious control or awareness.

Here are a few examples:

An American girl says "bloody" to her English fiancé and he explodes.

A boy, fresh from a liberal college campus, uses a crisp four letter classic in the presence of the protected minister's daughter and feels the psychic atmosphere turn cold.

Communication in Marriage

These are obvious conditionings. There are many, not so obvious, which may cause two people in love an endless amount of trouble if they don't investigate them, as a detective might, and expose their real meanings to each other.

You can usually tell when you are up against such an emotionally charged word by the response of your partner. Either the person freezes (blocks all expression of feeling) or discharges emotion wildly ("blows his top").

Blocking is easily discernible. A person may simply suck in his breath, stop talking, withdraw, change the subject, lose track of what he or she was about to say, or go off on a tangent quite unrelated to the topic in hand.

Over-discharge of feeling is even more apparent. A person may muster a whole regiment of rational arguments to defend an irrational position. A man may simply explode. A woman may burst into tears.

The thing to do is to stop the conversation right then and there and ask your partner, "What did I say that caused you distress?" Or, "I said something that made you withdraw. Please help our relationship out by telling me what it was." If loving communication is the goal (and it always needs to be the goal in marriage), this verbal snag must be removed from the path—or at least understood so that it can be bypassed.

In the case of the Englishman's reaction to the word "bloody," there is no problem. He can readily acknowledge the impact of cultural influence. The situation is not so clear when the affected person does not know why there has been such a reaction, or worse, cannot accept that he or she has over-reacted at all. However, that person does "feel uncomfortable" and somehow senses that there was something out of place about his or her reaction. With this as a starter, and with your help, confident that this will be free of reprisals the partner may be willing to trace down his or her associations to the troublesome word.

I believe that any two intelligent human beings who love each other can perform this service reciprocally, provided they observe a few "ground rules." These are simple, but they must be conscientiously adhered to. They consist of allowing the reactor to associate freely to the troublesome stimulus, asking again and again if necessary, "What comes to your mind as you think of the word ——?" The helper makes no comment except to offer an encouraging nod and a repetition of the original question, "And what else?" Under no circumstances may the helper become critical, judgmental, or evaluative—not even interpretive. His or her sole function is to hear, to receive, to encourage further associations by focusing attention on the stimulus. Any communications that emerge must be kept entirely confidential. That is all! The partner will make his or her own discoveries and experience a growing relief as the self is divested of an unsuspected load of *useless false conclusions*.

This technique, by the way, does not imply a complete psychoanalysis in one easy lesson. It is simply indicative of one among a number of ways that have been found to be useful to people in trouble.

Here is an example of how this might work:

The word is "babied."

A man says to his loved one, "I want to be babied tonight."

She recoils as if he had hit her. Outraged, she hurls at him, "I want a *man,* not a *baby!*"

He is hurt; she is angry. Clearly, they are in trouble unless he can overcome his pain long enough to remember that this girl has never refused him healing comfort when he needed it. There must be something else; something to do with his way of asking for what he wanted. He recalls that he has expressed similar needs to her before: "I need affection," "I need food," "I need petting," "I need you," reaching for her mothering roles, and she has given generously. But now, he has said, "I need to be babied," and the world falls apart.

It must be that word "babied."

Thoroughly alert to their dilemma, and no longer personally hurt, he invites her to consider the possibility that the word "babied" may contain implications for her that are painful and that he would like to understand them.

By this time, she, too, is aware that she has overreacted, and she is curious about this, a bit puzzled, and secretly grateful that she has a man who can be concerned for *her* rather than licking his own wounds like the baby she has accused him of being. He has clearly demonstrated himself a man, capable of clearheaded thinking; so she agrees to the search.

Presently, as the game gets under way, she uncovers a host of reactions to "babied" that explain her "irrational" fury. These are readily available to consciousness, but they have been stuffed away in memory's storehouse since she was a small girl. Even *she* is surprised at the emotion that still surrounds them. She discovers that "babied," to her, is associated with being rendered helpless, smothered, made useless, with loneliness, discomfort, bad smell, naughty, can't do it yourself, forced, rejection. Her "false emotional conclusions," formed early in childhood, at which time they were "true" for her, are that "babied" equals uselessness and rejection. No wonder her inner struggle to emancipate herself from this, and no wonder her panic when her lover wants her to "baby" him.

The old meanings begin to lose some of their power to control her as they come up from the underground. (A rule to remember is that anything repressed, shoved into the underground of consciousness, gains power and tends to act out of control.) Now she and her lover work out some new meanings, ones that she can experience pleasure from as she acts upon them. In other words, new conditioning, more appropriate to her life, is set up.

Time taken together in this way when the occasion demands avoids much heartache and is the essence of creative and constructive communication. These two lovers have laid an important building stone in their house of marriage—one that will stand the stress of time and make it possible for them to weather many another crisis.

Marital partners who are going to liberate each other to the sunlight of a loving relationship must learn to let their individual suns shine, each on the other. An atmosphere of frowning, like a black cloud, shadows and cools the warmth of their relationship. Disapproval of a loved person congeals that person *and* the atmosphere so that it may take time and special tender attention to thaw both.

Emotional growth comes about most readily in a climate of approval, just as plant growth takes place when there is sufficient warmth. Below certain temperatures, everything freezes, stops growing, stops moving, including communication between people. Even if we disapprove our spouse's activities, it helps not one whit to nag him or her about them. Nagging serves only to shut our partner off from us and may even reinforce the negative thing we dislike.

Suppose, for example, the husband is habitually late for dinner. Will it change his ways to complain about his lateness? Most wives would tell you it will not. Nor will it help, when he makes an isolated effort to get home one night on time, to greet him with, "Well! For once, you're here on time."

If change in his behavior is to come about at all, it will come as he feels warmed by her acceptance of him *as he is*, making him want, in turn, to satisfy her needs. When changes do come, they are helped by appreciation expressed by her.

Particularly destructive are those categorical descriptions that one spouse sometimes makes in the presence of the other or even to the other, such as, "He's lazy," or "She's sloppy," or "He'll never get ahead," or "He can't take a joke," or "She's stupid." Such phrases nail a living, mobile person to a rigid, unmoving structure.

At some point, each of us has to recognize that all living persons are beings struggling toward light as best they can. Like trees or plants, they reach upward, however gnarled and warped their exposed surfaces may appear. The chance that they have for reaching their full stature may well depend on how much warmth and nourishment they get and how little their natural impulses toward growth have been interfered with.

Your contribution to your mate may lie, not in hacking away at his or her behavior, but in bringing what approval you can to nourish the living being whom you profess to love, so that that person may grow in his or her own way toward a personal goal.

The verbal caress is one of the most effective aids I know. As the words imply, this is the touch of love, expressed verbally. The man who says, "I feel bathed in love when I am with you," or the woman who says, "Your courage gives me strength" are giving each other verbal caresses.

In our culture, where loved beings are physically separated from each other for so many hours of every day, we need singing words to affirm the reality of psychic closeness, even body closeness. These phrases stay with us for hours. They are more precious than money or affluence. In fact, we treasure them so highly that whenever we come across one in literature, we cling to it hungrily, pretending it was for us. The caressing words that some man has tendered his woman are chanted down the ages, and thousands of men and women feel their glow and are transformed. Somewhere there must be such an anthology for lovers. It could be a spark to kindle each man's and woman's own capacity for verbal caress.

We miss the best a person has to give us if we fail to make it possible for him or her to uncover daydreams. The Rainmaker (in the motion picture film of the same name) who transformed a woman's mundane life into a charmed existence by releasing her dream image of herself provided nourishment for her soul, however much he was unable to provide her with bread. We need bread with which to live, but it sticks in our throats without the wine of dreams to wash it down.

The release of daydreams carries us over into a land of enchantment that beckons irresistibly, and one fine day the boundaries of our present realities will get pushed out and onward in the direction of our dreams, for we might almost say that all happy reality starts in a dream.

But many of us are afraid to share a dream. We feel that we don't want to be held responsible for such nebulous beginnings, or that hidden facets of our personality may be laughed at or ridiculed, or that our embryonic hope may be made smaller and more unreal than it is. So we clam up, pretending that we never indulge in wishful fantasy, that daydreams are "for the birds."

How can we encourage our beloveds to share their dreams?

How can we break through their defensive shells so that their dreams and ours can light up our lives?

This is a sensitive undertaking, and we must be sure that we know how to "look," "listen," and "touch" without being destructive. A dream is as embryonic and may be as fragile as a newly sprouted seed or fertilized egg.

We might begin by being appreciative of our partner's expressed wishes, letting him or her know clearly that we approve of people having daydreams.

At some time a partner may speak of such a dream, though the expression of it may be almost inaudible, like a pebble dropped carelessly where no one can see it. But if we do see it, and express our wonder and approval, then the other person may take courage. He or she may protect himself or herself carefully while further testing our gentleness with dreams but, if he or she dares a bit, we could listen appreciatively. Perhaps we could ask questions that would expand the dream, but never those that could shrink it. If the dream is strong, and not too new the other person may invite us to play with it. If the romp is not too rough, he or she will doubtless venture further. Little by little it will be discovered that we are safe companions for dreams, and we will come to love them and understand him or her better because of them.

There are other kinds of dreams that are easier to share, partly, I suppose, because we don't feel so responsible for them. These are the night dreams, sometimes the night terrors. We are their makers, of course, though we may not realize it. These dreams are usually compounded of our wishes or our unresolved anxieties, and they constitute a kind of communication system between our so-called unconscious and our work-a-day conscious life. If we pay attention to them, particularly the repetitive ones and the night terrors, we may come closer to self-understanding. The best way to get at the significance of one's dream is to ask oneself what are one's associations to the various elements in it and to observe what the dream action is saying. In other words, what is the theme of the dream?

If your mate tells you a dream, you listen with interest. If you laugh at its incongruities, you laugh appreciatively. You never try to analyze your mate's dream, though you can sometimes ask questions that will help him or her to do so for himself or herself.

With a little practice, most of us can arrive at an

approximation of our own dream messages and, with it, a deeper understanding of the miraculous world of inner space.

We call our times "the age of the discovery of outer space." But my conviction is that the world of outer space holds nothing like the wonders and adventures of each person's inner world.

8
The Wall of Moodiness

The other side of the coin of communication is moodiness. Silence, like a curtain, draws down around a couple, shutting off one partner from the other. Gone is the quiet companionship of warm, unspoken thoughts. A wall is erected that neither can penetrate or climb over. Occasionally, it approximates hate, though they hardly dare admit this, even privately, each to himself or herself. It leaves them helpless and cold, and neither knows how to reach the other.

The colder each gets, the more paralyzed with fear each becomes. Perhaps they think that they shouldn't have married after all. Out of panic, they may do or say something nasty which precipitates a real quarrel, which, at least, restores to them some kind of contact. Yet if this goes on, their marriage may end in divorce.

Is there any way that these moody spells can be kept from spoiling their relationship? Is there some step that either could take to dispel them when they come? I think that there is.

The coldness, the paralysis that a wife or a husband feels

in the presence of the partner's moodiness is probably akin to the way *that* partner felt in the moments preceding the mood. Something happens; something is communicated or left uncommunicated; some meaning is attached to circumstance or deed which, for reasons not apparent, paralyzes expression of feeling and, in turn, stops all communication.

Moodiness is frozen feeling, emotion paralyzed in its expression, held tight instead of flowing freely. A person in its grip isolates himself or herself upon the beachhead of a lonely little island, defended like a fortress, even from the beloved.

What makes feelings freeze? What inhibits their expression? What can be done about it? The following illustration of one couple's encounter with moodiness may provide some answers to these questions.

"How can I ever understand Tim if he just freezes up and won't talk to me?" Jean asked in despair, after she and her husband had endured an evening of stony silence. "When I see him grow rigid like that I might as well try to communicate with a fence post as with him. The next thing I know, my own mind starts playing hob with me. I imagine all the possible and impossible things I might have done to offend him or wonder what awful things might have happened to him during the day. Then I get so worried that I say all the wrong things. I keep wishing that he could tell me what *is* going on inside him."

"Jean," I answered, "you may not realize it, but he *has* given you the essential clues to his feelings. Of course, you didn't understand the language that he used to tell you about them because, until recently, no one has known very much about it. You did, however, notice Tim's body tensions, even though your attention was concentrated on his silence. Actually, he spoke eloquently to you."

The Wall of Moodiness

"What do you mean?" she interrupted. "He was as uncommunicative as a log and as tight as a drum. When he did speak to me, it was in monosyllables."

"That's exactly the point, Jean. He was immobilized by fear. Consciously or unconsciously, he dreaded the imagined consequences of expressing his feelings. So he braced himself against the movement of feeling (emotion), and you interpreted his resultant rigidity as unwillingness to communicate with you. In addition, you concluded that the only things which could make him so unwilling were disapproval of you or that something tragic had happened during his day. It would help you and Tim if you both learned a bit about the physical and emotional manifestations of moodiness and the curious language of muscle tensions, as well as why people have become so afraid of relaxing them."

Jean settled herself to listen. Her problem was one that is faced by thousands of young couples who are terrorized by immobility and silence in their loved ones. Their common plea is, "If only my partner could *talk* to me and tell me what the matter is!"

I told Jean that we are not born "stiffs." On the contrary, at birth we are highly mobile, with the ability to cry, to rage, to enjoy pleasurable sensations. We have built-in equipment for responding feelingfully to life experiences. Our emotions are simply nothing more than feelings *in motion* and are expressed in appropriate bodily activity. The movement itself is a human being's healthy way of dealing with joy, sadness, frustration, and fear.

However, people have not always understood the value or the function of this potential. In ignorance, they have denied the right and the need of feelings to move. They have even called the mobility "bad" because, in its raw form, they have viewed it as being something powerful and dangerous. Accordingly, they have sought to curb it, often by punishment. The most effective and severe punishment was disapproval and isolation of the child who expressed his feelings. "Put him in his crib and let him cry it out." "Big boys don't cry." "Nice little girls don't get angry." "Good little children don't touch themselves."

When a child is thus reprimanded for the expression of feelings, he or she gradually learns to inhibit such expression. Because all emotion normally results in some kind of bodily action, there is only one way a person can inhibit emotion, namely, by muscularly stopping its normal movement.

"What do you mean?" Jean asked, surprised. "I thought we controlled our feelings with our minds."

"We direct their expression with our brains, but we actually effect the 'stop' or 'go' of the movement in the musculature of our bodies. Let us suppose, Jean, that you were angry. What would you guess might be some primary ways in which your anger would want to be expressed through you body?"

"Well," pondered Jean, "I'd want to hit, or punch, or scratch, or kick, or bite, or scream."

"Good for you! These ways of reacting to anger-provoking situations are so well recognized that we have even coined phrases to describe the body sensations we experience. We say, 'I was so mad I could have bitten his head off.' 'I wanted to poke his nose in.' 'I'd like to throw her out the window.' 'I'd like to kick him right into kingdom come.' 'I was so furious that I could have screamed.' What do you suppose our muscles do when they want to move in these ways in response to anger-provoking situations and we cannot permit them to do so?"

"They stiffen."

"Of course. The conscious or unconscious fear is that if we permit them to move in any way at all 'something terrible may happen,' with horrible consequences. In other

The Wall of Moodiness

words, the desolation of the punished child is triggered and activated. In the adult, the whole repressive mechanism of muscular inhibition of movement that was learned and developed ever since that first encounter with reprimand or punishment for expressing emotions then goes into high gear. The result is tightness of those muscles normally utilized in the expression of anger. It takes a lot of energy to maintain a hold on muscles that are straining to perform their natural function. Emotion cannot be entirely shut off, however, or the result is some form of physical or emotional distress of a more serious nature.

"Let's take a look at your Tim now. We'll suppose that on his way home to you someone pushed him out of line at the supermarket; someone else edged him away from the door of the bus at the stop so that he had to ride a couple of extra blocks; and then, to top it all, a cop bawled him out for crossing the street against the light. Let us also suppose that your Tim is one of those 'good little boys' who have been taught to repress feeling. He arrives home with an immobilizing tension in his right shoulder, his biceps, and the back of his neck, which you can spot from across the room. (That is, you can spot it if you know how to look.) In the past half hour his fist has needed to fly out at least three times before he ever arrived on your doorstep. Now you greet him with a, 'Darling, before you take your coat off, will you empty the garbage can?' An innocent enough request, but he, at the explosion point, answers you by gritting his teeth even harder and going out with the can in stony silence.

"His unconscious terror, you must remember, is that 'something awful might happen' if he let his muscles move the way they want and need to move. If asked why he couldn't 'let himself go' a bit, he would rationalize by saying, 'A man must control his temper,' or 'If I give way to my feelings, I might well knock down a wall.' It never occurs to him, of course, that he could let his feelings *move* without there being any damage to man or property.

"Naturally, Jean, he is not in a position to talk with you in any relaxed manner, let alone affectionately. If you had observed the set of his jaw, the tension in his neck and shoulders, his clenched fists, or the thrust of his leg as it planted itself firmly on the floor to avoid kicking the kitchen door as he went out, you would have known that Tim was suffering an explosive need to let off steam. You would not have intensified the pressure; nor would you have felt defensive if he shut you out of his consciousness while he used his energy to immobilize his own rage. You didn't know this, of course, and so you began to feel guilty and troubled. Because no one can stand guilt, you grew tense and you worsened the situation by becoming critical of yourself. Tim was not in a position to exchange affectionate responses with anyone; not until he had worked off his anger. But the tragedy was that Tim didn't know how to work off anger, nor did he guess that he could have done it with impunity.

"One of the problems with our society is that there doesn't seem to be enough physical ways to blow off steam so that we may release ourselves from these anger tensions, and civilized people don't seem to have enough imagination or grasp of the problem to invent any. An uninhibited shout, a bang on a bed, a pillow slung against a blank wall, a brisk walk around the block would serve admirably to discharge them. So would massage of the neuromuscular spasms in the back of the neck and upper shoulders. These knots of tension are created when people impede the natural movement of anger feelings. Deep breathing could also help, with attention to full exhalation.

"Now let's go back to the problem of your learning how to interpret other muscular tensions in Tim. You saw how his body looked when he was holding on to anger. You noticed his tight shoulders, his set jaws, his tense legs, his clenched fists. If you had happened to touch the muscular spasm in his shoulders, he would have cried 'Ouch!' Suppose that instead of being exposed to an anger-provoking situation he had met with a very sad one. What do you think would be a person's normal bodily reaction to sorrow?"

"He'd want to cry, I suppose, or maybe even sob."

"Of course. You, being a woman, might be free to do just that. But Tim, being a man, was made ashamed when his feelings moved in this healthy way. 'A man doesn't cry' is the inviolable commandment to the Anglo-Saxon male child. Later, when life situations come along to sadden him, involuntarily he tightens those very muscles that need to express sadness. This inhibition takes effort, and his tension mounts. He swallows down his sobs, stiffens his spine, sets his jaw, keeps a stiff upper lip. It takes so much of his vital energy to maintain immobility of feeling that the result is a muscular stasis with almost total rigidity. Here again, his unconscious terror (stemming from childhood) is that if he loses his grip on his feelings 'something terrible may happen.'

"The muscles in his upper mid back which normally would be called into play if he gave way and sobbed are taut as bowstrings. He does not 'feel like' eating his dinner because his diaphragm is so contracted that digestion is interfered with. His throat is so tight that he feels as if food couldn't get through it. A good look at Tim would tell you the story.

"Tim, of course, needs to learn that God gave him the ability to cry as a means of laying down the burden of sorrow; that there is nothing unmanly about tears; and that the strongest and bravest of men become stronger and braver and more enduring when they give way and cry for just cause. In addition, expression of his sadness would bring him into healthy and compassionate communication with you who love him. But you, Jean, may have a tough job persuading him of this. However, if you have correctly perceived the muscle-tension language, you may succeed in releasing his immobilizing rigidity by gently placing your warm, caressing hand on his throat, or by massaging his back in the area where neuromuscular spasms occur as a result of held-back sadness. (To locate these, draw an imaginary line around the body beginning at the diaphragm. It would bisect those spasms in the back just to the left and right of the spinal column.)

"For a long time, in my own professional work, I experimented with ways to help people to cry. Often, I could literally *see* their need to weep, and almost hear their sobs, but the sound was noiseless and their eyes were dry while their chests were held as tight as drums. I would suggest, 'Go ahead and cry. It takes a brave man to expose his grief.' Sometimes this worked; but often it did not. Gradually, I learned that if I acknowledged something fine and wonderful about the person while laying my hand over the tight and tense area of the throat, and if I massaged the neuromuscular spasms in his back, tears would soon flow freely, often accompanied by wracking sobs. Within minutes, he would feel relaxed, refreshed, and ready to 'carry on.' Miraculously, at this point, he was also ready for verbal communication.

"Wives & husbands who see, acknowledge, and act upon the muscle-language communications release feelings that *need* to move, and they thus restore their partners to a healthy mobility, making other forms of communication possible.

"Now, Jean, what about fear and anxiety? How do you think a person's body would behave in fear?"

"Well, I get cold feet," she replied.

"Exactly, and no doubt you get cold hands also."

"Yes, and I feel tied up in knots right here (pointing to

The Wall of Moodiness

her solar plexus), and sometimes I have to go to the bathroom."

"Of course, in anxiety and fear you are likely to contract all over, to stiffen all over. You also inhibit your breathing; hence the tied-up-in-knots sensation you describe. Eventually, you may start to swallow air, because you will also be suffering from oxygen starvation. Most people raise their arms and clasp their hands behind their heads, which seems to them like a more comfortable way to resist full breathing while bracing themselves from perception of their own anxiety. These manifestations, along with a cold skin temperature, are your clues.

"Now let us suppose that your Tim is worried, though he hasn't been able to talk to you about it as yet. You note that his hands are like ice. He heads for the cocktail department for quick warmth. He plays with the dinner you've prepared so painstakingly and then later on nibbles maddeningly from the icebox.

"Whatever you may think, he is *not* trying to imply that you are a bad cook. He *is* saying that he is suffering from anxiety. It will probably not help to ask outright what worries him unless he already has developed full confidence in your willingness to listen without criticism, in which case he will have started to talk as soon as you have given him a chance. It *will* help to rub his back or to take his hands in yours and warm them, and his feet also. A cup of hot tea is a blessing. These ministrations, along with an attitude of complete acceptance, will soothe him, and presently, as he thaws, he may want to talk about his anxiety.

"It is well to remember that whenever any of us is confronted with the evidence of neuromuscular spasms in another (cramped tightnesses from prolonged inhibition of feeling), these should be recognized as screams for help. They are a communication to you that the other person is in trouble and needs help in getting out of it.

"We feel good when we find acceptable ways to permit

our feelings to move. What is more, we are then able to manage the stresses and strains of living more effectively and with less wear and tear, less susceptibility to self-destroying bouts of moodiness. A lover who can detect the need for movement of feeling in his or her mate and who can find ways to release it is saving heartache for them both. What is more, this is opening the door to communication between them and is adding years to the life-span of the beloved."

There are other sources of moodiness (frozen feeling) that arise within the marital relationship itself. We might look at some of these.

Perhaps a man tries to tell his wife something and she doesn't hear it. Or if she hears, she doesn't seem to pay attention, or she brushes it off as silly, unimportant, or insignificant. Or, he may make his communication in a disarmingly offhand or joking way, minimizing its real importance to him.

Most of us have had too little experience in listening to another person with full attention. Often what we hear are *words,* and we miss the emotional *meanings* behind the words. Hearing intuitively is an art almost undeveloped in our culture, yet our own deep longing is to have someone hear us in this way. When the person whom we love fails to respond to our emotional communications, we may be thrown into a despair somewhat like the desolation of the very young child who first discovers that he or she cannot reach the mother.

The husband, for example, undoubtedly *wants* to reach his wife, but his feeling may be that he cannot, that if he tries she will not understand. The dynamics of this reaction were set in motion long ago, when he was truly a helpless infant and he reached and did not find, again and again. The anguish of those occasions was so acutely painful that he began to protect himself with a shell (habit) of "I won't care," "I won't feel."

The wife's job, in this case, is to show her husband that she is a safe person to reach toward; that she will make an effort to hear; and that when she fails, her failure is not of intent but of personal limitation, which she will work to change, which both can work to change. She might start by assuming that somehow she has shut him off. She could tell him that she feels this to be the case; that she doesn't know what she did but that she wants to find out. She could affirm again that it is her heart's desire to hear everything he wants to tell her, to respond to his feelings with full understanding.

Even this may not suffice if his original hurt was deep and habitual, for the tendency is to disbelieve that anyone *wants* to heal his emotional pain and to react against what he may falsely assume to be pity. He may have been encouraged to hope and to reach tentatively. But the reach may have been so half-way that it went unrecognized and unresponded to, and the very hint of failure has thrown him despondently back into the frustration experienced as a child.

Her words will register, however, if not at the moment, then presently; especially if her tone of voice is really "seeking" and if he is sure that she is nonjudgmental or accusatory. Perhaps he will open up a little. Certanly he wants to, but *dare* he really trust her? This is a critical moment for them both, for her own tendency may be to become defensive. All she really needs to do now is to hear him and assure him that what she hears makes it possible for her to love him more completely, more wisely. There is time enough later to tell him of the way the situation looked from where she viewed it. When some of the pain of *his* inhibition is washed away, when the ice is melted, he may ask her to fill in the details of her own experience so that he may understand the what and the why of the situation for *her*.

Another source of moodiness (frozen feeling) is anger or displeasure with the mate that is held in tight; that dares not find expression in the presence of the beloved for fear one will be punished or rejected.

Perhaps a wife has reproved her husband for such expressions by withdrawing her demonstrations of affection for a time. For instance, suppose that he has remonstrated with her for having lunch with an old beau and she has responded by refusing to kiss him goodnight. Or she may have found some other way to hurt him as she worked off her own fury at his seeming lack of trust.

This is a big price for him to pay for exposing his feeling of anger, stemming from jealousy. Next time he'll hold it in. The result—moodiness. Now she'll wonder why she cannot penetrate the wall.

What she might do in a case like this is to tell him that she is glad that he can share his angry jealousy with her, that she wants to expose feeling experienced by either of them, not to shut it off. Then she might tell him that her old friends have contributed a great deal to making her the woman he now loves. That she would like to share friends with him wherever they can still contribute to the marriage. That some of them may still need her special concern for their own sakes, but that he need not worry about an erotic attachment, because the full flow of her love is channeled toward him.

Little by little, he may be able to tell her why he "saw red" when this particular "old friend" went out of the way to meet her. Or why other men or women in her life make him feel insecure. Together they will find some way to build his sense of security so that their relationship can contain many warm friendships, male and female, which will bring richness and variety to their home.

Another source of moodiness is damaged self-feeling.

The Wall of Moodiness

When a person is made to experience himself (or herself) as inadequate by the beloved capacity to express oneself at all in the presence of the other is injured.

Let us suppose, for example, that a couple is in a social gathering. The husband listens attentively to every other woman, but when his wife starts to talk, he interrupts, or in some apparently small, depreciatory way, makes her feel less than good about herself. (This dilemma may occur when a man lacks self-confidence and unwittingly subjects his wife to conformity to his *own* pattern of false modesty. His manner with her reflects his own self-depreciatory attitudes.) Nevertheless, depreciation in any form is so painful that, rather than risk its discomfort, a woman (or man) may become silent (moody) in those circumstances which have called it forth.

The husband's task, in this instance, is to restore to his wife some good feelings about herself; to appreciate her communications, both in public and in private; and to celebrate her to his friends in her presence in ways that please her.

Sometimes one partner makes a promise to the other that he or she has no serious intention of keeping. It was born from a momentary impulse of generosity and then irresponsibly forgotten.

To the promised one, however, it holds a world of cherished meaning. It is taken into mind and heart and around it are built all manner of unrealistic fantasies. Because of what one "makes" of it, one is left "wide open," vulnerable and exposed, like a child at Christmas who erroneously believes that Santa Claus has invited him or her to ask for the improbable.

Then the day of reckoning comes. The promise is unkept and the dreamer of dreams feels exploited, cheated, unloved; and closes up. The fear is that the lover can no longer be trusted. Yet one cannot fully admit this, even to oneself. On the one hand, the idea is too horrendous, and also not entirely true. On the other hand, he or she knows that a dream castle was built on hope more than on promise.

What is this couple to do? The breaker of the promise is hardly aware that damage has been done until he or she collides with the mate's hurt, solid, stolid silence. How is one to penetrate this silence when he or she is not about to expose the self further by confessing the predicament?

There is one act, at least, that one can start with. When a man (or a woman) is faced with frozen feeling in someone loved, a warming, thawing assurance of love is in order, no matter what the cause. No one is moody when he or she feels good about himself or herself, feels loved and able to let feelings move. A wife may need rescuing from her own painful constructions and interpretations of her husband's failure to meet her need and vice versa.

Perhaps all it will take is the simple statement from him that he must have done something thoughtless and unintended which has hurt her, and if so, will she tell him about it; will she give him a chance to repair the damage? This may bring a torrent of repressed feeling from her, and with it, a flow of love that has been painfully dammed.

When they can once more talk freely with each other, she will need to tell him how much she counts on certain kinds of promises and how far afield her mind travels with them. He, in turn, will probably learn from this experience to think twice before he makes an idle promise that he cannot keep. Nowhere does the truth matter so much as it does between two persons in love. Every woman wants to feel that her husband is as good as his word and every man wants to feel that his wife is as good as her word. In this world of shaky verities, we crave contact with at least one human being who can be depended upon to keep one's word.

The Wall of Moodiness

Moodiness, then, is inhibited (frozen) feeling, usually associated with unreceived communications; or with unexpressed anger, fear or sorrow; or with damaged self-feeling; or with some undermining of the trust relationship. It does, indeed, feel like a wall, or at least a curtain, shutting out the beloved. A destructive attack, ending in a quarrel, will bring the couple contact, but will not bring them love.

If they wish to remove the stones from the wall—in other words, restore the flow of warm, contactful feeling between them—it will require an effort on the part of each to receive the communications of the other, to permit the negative feelings of each some expression without punishment, to repair the damage to self that was unwittingly inflicted, to restore an atmosphere of trust. This is healing that provides room for emotional growth. It is also part of the architecture of love.

9
Sexual Artistry

Partners in love are originally drawn to each other precisely because they are sexual beings. They go on being entranced with each other to the degree that positive sexuality continues to remain alive between them. This is not to imply that other enduring virtues don't matter. They do, but it is in the fullness of sexual expression that these are enhanced and enriched.

A sexually sophisticated man once said "Most men come home to go to bed: but when I go to bed I come home." His attitude expressed that of happily committed lovers, for when two such persons offer their bodies for each other's enjoyment, they are giving of the very essence of personal treasure. To each, this is home.

One definition of sex is "the power to unite the separated." Sexual communication becomes, then, the energy in one body seeking union with the energy in another, each coming home to the other.

Healthy, free-flowing sexual communication, which seems so effortless to the naive, is actually the result of superb skill, acquired through informed practice, and of superb character, acquired through ethical action. Though we are born sexual beings, we are not born artists in the use of sex, any more than we are born artists of speech.

To start with, there is magic power in caressing words. These act hynotically for good and tend to bring about the very responses they suggest. This is especially true of those that express appreciative enjoyment of the sexual organs themselves. There is a deeply transforming effect on a man when his beloved can express her reverence for his penis, who is genuinely excited by its movement from flaccidity to erection in response to her; who loves its velvety touch against her hand, her cheek, her breast; who feels that whatever part of her body receives it comes alive and is fulfilled. And the juices flow in a woman whose lover tells her of his delight in the beauty of her genitality. Such attitudes, cultivated, believed, and reciprocated, lead to inner and outer beauty. Skin feels alive, tone is evident, eyes sparkle, and an allover joyousness is experienced. As these miracles occur, a person communicates vitality and radiance—and also communicates sex. In the deepest biblical sense man and woman *know* each other.

In the language of the body the act of touch, when freed of all destructive tension, says to the beloved "you are liked." Everyone knows that people reach out to touch that which pleases them and recoil from that which displeases them. Most of us are hungrily searching for evidence from others that we are likable, so when someone gives us the simple gift of touch approval, it comes to us as healing. Healing, too, is the relaxation that follows in the wake of any pleasurable sensory stimulation. There are nerve endings of pleasure all over our skin surfaces. When these are touched tenderly, our response is to draw closer, to lay down our defenses, to open ourselves to communication with the toucher.

Incidentally, a person can usually tell when his or her

own hands will feel good to another by the radiant warmth that is experienced in them. If, in bringing the palms together, one feels a kind of tingling aliveness that seems to flow from one hand to the other just before they meet, they are likely to feel warming to someone else. They will also be in a state of readiness for the giving and receiving of touch communications.

Hands will only feel like this when a person is able to breathe so that every exhalation brings with it a pleasurable streaming sensation throughout the whole body. This means 'letting go' all over. Breathing will not be full and free if there is any muscular tightness anywhere. In other words, a body must be in a state of alive awareness (alert relaxation) if it is to generate the warming glow that is perceived by another as so very regenerative. It is for this reason that sex counselors today are incorporating some training in massage into the instruction of couples. This is often called training in sensate focus which simply means learning to give attention, thru caressing touch, to other parts of the body than those specifically involved with sex.

Furthermore, the touch of sex for sex's sake, for the specific arousal of sexual response, accomplishes its goal to the degree that the toucher is sensitively aware of what is touched. So many lovers, male and female, suffer from mechanistic heavy-handedness or from psychic disconnectedness from their own organs of touch. This unfeeling laying on of hands produces the opposite of sexual communication.

A lover who wants to convey love needs to allow the mind and the spirit to go down and live in the hand that touches. It is, after all, the bridge of communication over which, through which, passes his or her devotion. It must enjoy the changing conditions of moisture, the throbbing movement developing with the emergence of excitation. The hand itself must leap to its experience as a bee is drawn to an opening flower if the touch of love is to feel good to the beloved. This is true for both men and for women. Neither derives pleasure from dead-hand, rigid, or mechanical approaches.

Many persons find it hard to keep two moving organisms in focus at once. Yet, this is almost exactly what accomplished sexual communicants learn to do. Usually, a beginner (or even a more experienced lover not yet fully aroused) may need to focus on the self until orgasm is reached. Then the process may be reversed and the focus put upon the other. This is much like a pianist who practices with the right hand and then with the left and only then is able to blend them together in harmonious sound.

Mutual orgasm is the glorious sound of such a duet. Any orgasm, however, whether duo or solo, is perceived as a creative phenomenon. Blessed by love, its psychic effect is creativity on every level. Sometimes it results in the birth of a baby, but nearly always it results in a renewed and optimistic vision of life. The communicants feel transformed, a bit nearer heaven, a bit more aware of the potential of humanity.

Lovers need to free themselves from their fear of reaching for love. Most people suffer from the conviction that they will be desolate if they reach out and are not responded to. This conviction, of course, springs from built-in, but long forgotten, memories of those times when they were helpless infants and were unable to satisfy their own needs—when they reached and nobody was there. What few people realize, as adults, is the profound pleasure there actually is in 'reach' for its own sake. Of course there is no denying the ecstasy of having one's reach responded to. But in adult life, reaching itself, whether responded to or not, leaves one more whole as a person than one would be by withholding the expression of longing. Furthermore, there need be no devastation if one is occasionally denied.

A temporary 'no' is not necessarily a permanent rejection. And besides, every resourceful adult has many ways to satisfy any need that may be experienced.

Many women like to be talked to when they are being made love to. Perhaps this is their need to be reassured. Or perhaps it may be the engrossing hypnotic effect of positive suggestion that helps her to focus her mind on lovemaking rather than on the distractions of pleasure anxiety (guilty response to good feelings in one's body) or on the fear of failure; but whatever the undercurrent, she is likely to say "Talk to me. Tell me that you love me and that it doesn't matter how long it takes me to come to orgasm."

It is strange how few men are able to appreciate and act upon this need. Though men, seemingly by nature, are the talkers of this world, in bed many of them become curiously dumb, as if embarassed to use the words of love.

Some women bewilder men (and also themselves) by the cyclical nature of their sexual drive. These females are as wildly sexual for a part of the month as an animal in heat, and otherwise are as cool as cucumbers and couldn't be less interested in sex. This is often just as bothersome to the woman as it is to her partner, who may find it very hard to adjust to. Sometimes hormones help when the mood swing of a woman veers toward profound depression. Oftentimes during the 'low' days before menstruation, lovemaking might better take the form of cuddling and back rubs for her and noncoital forms of lovemaking for him, such as petting to orgasm.

One quirk of human nature is the irrational assumption that a person who loves one 'ought' to know one's sexual needs and that one 'ought' never have to verbalize these at all. The partner 'should' be able to anticipate them in every detail.

The partner's reaction to such an assumption is "I'm no mind reader. I would love to satisfy you if you ask outright for what you want, but I can't be expected to guess these wants." And he or she might well like to add "And I'd like you to act pleased when I do give you what you want."

When one asks, one risks, of course, and the fear of rejection goes very deep. I have heard many a woman say, for example "I asked him once, but he forgets and I'll be darned if I am going to keep on telling him what I like." And then she goes underground and becomes moody when she doesn't get the kind or the amount of sexual stimulation that she needs. The fact that it may take him a while to catch on and that he may have to be told several different times in different ways never occurs to her. She simply assumes that forever after it doesn't pay to ask for what she wants, or she erroneously concludes that her man doesn't love her.

There are men, of course, who never do learn, and furthermore, never want to learn. But they are not the partners found in a loving relationship.

Many a man asks "How can I convince my partner that it is as much up to her to make love to me as it is for me to make love to her?"

Some women in our culture are still being stupidly conditioned to believe that theirs is the role of the sought after. This persists even into marriage and other kinds of committed relationships, even after they have been 'found'.

Although there are a few men who do resent having the woman initiate a sexual lovemaking episode, most men enjoy this greatly. It is as much a compliment to a man that a woman of his choice desires him sexually as it is a pleasure to a woman when a man desires her.

Sometimes I have heard women say "I asked him once and he didn't want sex, so I have never asked him again." This overreaction to an imagined rebuf is based on utterly nonsensical reasoning. How many times might the same woman have said to him "I'm tired tonight," or "I don't feel like it now."

If she is honest with herself, she may remember how often she herself has responded to seduction. Why must she conclude, when the roles are reversed, that her lover is incapable of similar seduction? Men delight in this as do women. A man might let his partner know very early in their relationship that he will welcome her taking the initiative. If, on some special occasion, he feels really disinclined, he can say something like this "You're a dear for wanting to make love to me, but I'm really not 'with it' tonight. Let me take a rain check now, but make sure you ask me again."

If, on the other hand, either partner perceives that the other is already tremendously sexually eager and excited, it is wise to see to it that that one comes to orgasm in some way—if not by intercourse, then by some noncoital means.

This brings up another matter frequently faced by partners, namely, that of frequency of lovemaking. Many couples wonder what is normal, and often this causes arguments and hurt feelings. There is tremendous individual variation in the matter of sexual energy. Some persons can enjoy sexual activity three times a day seven days a week. We sometimes speak of these as our sexual athletes. There are others who are content with sex once a month—in fact they feel violated if induced to participate more often. Imagine the problems that arise when a person of high sexual energy becomes deeply involved with someone of low sexual desire. It is in this discrepancy that many of the most serious lover's rows occur, and some relationships eventually break up over it. Contrary to past opinion, the more eager partner may just as likely be the woman as the man. In fact, a woman of high sexual energy can outdo even the most sexually energetic man, just as a woman of low sexual desire can be more passive than the least sexy man. In other words, the range is greater in the female than in the male.

Sexual Artistry

It goes without saying that it is tremendously important to a harmonious relationship that two persons be reasonably well matched in this matter of sexual drive; otherwise they will have to become unusually adept at finding satisfying solutions, or they will be in constant trouble. A good principle to remember is that it is essential to pay attention to the needs of the more eager partner. This does not have to be accomplished thru intercourse. In fact, intercourse need not be (and should not be) forced on anyone. But petting a partner to orgasm need be no more demanding of the less eager partner than rubbing a back or doing any one of a number of other personal acts of love.

Without such release of sexual tension, frustration can build to volcanic proportions. This is one aspect of sexuality that requires the utmost frankness. Again I emphasize that couples need to communicate their needs to each other without fear of rebuff. Ingenious couples find ways to satisfy each other's hunger even when one or the other does not feel like personal physical involvement.

It is particularly important not to let the eager partner feel that his or her high sexual endowment is a bad thing or in any way abnormal, for it is not. When ill-informed persons call their partners "satyrs" or "nymphmomniacs" they are simply defining someone who is more highly sexually endowed than they are. I have known of many relationships that were utterly destroyed because the poorly endowed person tried to make the richly endowed one feel guilty or as if he or she were a misfit.

So rejoice in high endowment, and if your partner has more than you, find an outlet for its expression without wearing you out.

Some persons ask "If my partner doesn't seem to want sex any more when once it was most desired, does that mean that I am no longer loved?"

The answer, of course, is no. Lack of desire where it

previously existed may be due to many causes. Some persons, for example, who become deeply involved in provocative and anxiety-creating occupations seem to lose all sexual desire for a time. I have seen those who, subjected to high-pressure business enterprises in exhausting cities like New York, lose their desire for sex, but gain it again when on vacation and freed from pressure.

It is quite possible, of course, for lack of sexual desire to mean lack of interest, which in turn may have come about because a partner was neither stimulated intellectually nor nourished emotionally. When any person, man or woman, who under ordinary circumstances has been an ardent lover suddenly ceases to be, it is well to examine the possible psychological reasons for the disinterest. Perhaps there is a feeling of not being appreciated; perhaps there is fatigue; perhaps there is someone else, though in this case, a partner is more apt to be a better lover than a worse one since the presence of another sexually stimulating person tends to generate a burst of sexual energy which is transferred to the stable relationship as well as flowing to the new lover. In any event, this is a time to take a new and fresh look at one's partner, giving him or her all the appreciation and other evidences of love of which one is capable.

Some human beings are more needful of adventure than others, but almost any sexual relationship can become bogged in boring and repetitive sexual routines. If one's own imagination is blocked, erotic literature and films may open up new vistas. Fortunately some fine examples of both are available today. (See appendix for notations of titles and where to find them.)

Wherever love and imagination exist, it is not too hard to find one's way into the wonderland of sexual fun. But a badly conditioned adult may have to be reassured again and again that good lovers around the world have done such things as make love in unorthodox places—the living room,

Sexual Artistry

the shower, beside a stream in broad daylight—that they enjoy mouth-genital activity and dozens of other kinds of sexual expression. In fact, any sexual act that is a pleasure to both partners is normal. The sky is the limit with a stop sign only for that which is painful or unpleasant to one or the other. One of the continuing joys of sex is its variety of manifestation.

Men frequently ask "What can I do to help the woman I love to enjoy sex more and to want it more?"

While there are women who don't seem to have very much sexual drive, most of the women who have become disinterested are, in truth, highly sexual beings who have become frustrated too often because sexual stimulation for them has not culminated in orgasm. One can hardly expect any woman to enjoy sex for very long or to want it very frequently if it ends in such misery. Usually such a state can be remedied. Women can learn how to come to orgasm, and men can be taught how to be adept lovers.

This leads us, of course, to the most common question that women themselves ask about sex: "How can I learn to come to orgasm?"

Tomes have been written in response to this question, but the following points seem to me to be the critical ones in establishing ease of orgasm for women.

First, a woman must recognize the elementary relationship of stimulus to response. Her richest abundance of nerve endings of pleasure lies in the area of her clitoris (meaning 'the key'). These nerve endings need continuous stimulation (stroking, caressing, touching) right up to the moment of orgasm.

Too often this has been called 'foreplay', with the assumption that there is something better to come.

It is helpful here to think of an analogy. To have light in an electric lamp one must connect a plug and turn on the switch. As long as the connection is not interfered with, there is light. But if the plug is pulled, the light goes out. Much the same thing happens in sexual excitation. As long as the nerve endings surrounding the clitoris are being stimulated, the result is mounting sexual pleasure which eventually results in orgasm. But when that stimulus is removed, the response generally stops. The insertion of the penis in no way substitutes for continuing stimulation of the clitoris. This is hard for many men to grasp. They utilize excellent stimulatory techniques until a woman becomes excited. Then they mistakenly "pull the plug" by transferring from manual or oral clitoral stimulation to penile penetration without clitoral contact. This is the equivalent of disconnecting the power source. The same men wonder why the woman's sexual excitation turns off. Quite naturally, she loses sensation at the very moment when she needs it most, and her near orgasm recedes, leaving her with congestion and discomfort in the entire pelvic area. She is then in a mood generally described as 'bitchy'. Had her lover continued his 'foreplay' to the very start of orgastic release, she would probably have experienced orgasm. Furthermore, she could comfortably enjoy and tolerate his coming to orgasm through penetration thereafter—probably sharing a second orgasm with him.

The false notion that orgasm must be experienced at the same moment has precipitated many a man into premature penile entry. Women are partly to blame for this, because their longing to feel something inside them often causes them to give their lovers false signals, urging them to "come inside" before they are really "over the hill" as it were.

A simple solution is for the man to enter at the beginning of love play, then to slip over onto his side, slightly at right angles to the woman. This permits him free use of his hand while he rests comfortably for whatever length of time it may take to excite her sufficiently for orgasm. Furthermore, his penis becomes well aware of her mounting tension and is already in place and responding. In this way, they have a very good chance of simultaneous orgasm if this is their great desire. However, simultaneous orgasm in general, represents an occasional 'peak' experience that is delightful but not necessary.

Once the orgasm reflex is well established, some women learn to undulate their own hips in response to the pelvic thrust of their lovers, so that the clitoris gets sufficient stimulation from penile friction alone. However, most women continue to need considerable manual stimulation right up to the moment of orgasm.

Learning to masturbate successfully is an important first step for a woman who is training herself to come to orgasm. Many a woman refuses to do this, exclaiming indignantly "Why should I do this to myself when I have a man to make love to me!" The fact remains, however, that no one should expect another to engage in a sexual dance until he or she has learned at least to walk. Also, many men tire after forty-five minutes or so of continuous clitoral stimulation, and this may very well be the time that it will take an untrained woman to reach climax. Her own willingness to educate herself may make the difference between a woman able to come to orgasm with her lover and one who cannot.

When starting practice in masturbation, make sure the clitoral area is well lubricated. Cold cream, K.Y. jelly, or any water soluble lubricant will do. Saliva from the mouth is just fine. Reading erotic literature for a while first or reading the erotic fantasies of other women (see appendix) are great stimulants, perhaps the best. Take it slow and easy and discover what is fun. Sexual imagination is one of the keys to sexual fulfillment.

If manual methods do not work at first, try a vibrator. There are a number on the market today (see appendix) some powered by flashlight batteries and some electronically powered. The latter are most powerful but the former are gentler. Which a woman prefers is a matter of individual taste.

Some therapists feel that because a vibrator is so stimulating no penis could produce a sensation to match it. A woman may become addicted to the vibrator and forget the joys of the penis. This doesn't seem to be borne out by fact, however. When a man and woman love each other they often use the vibrator to bring the woman to her first orgasm, then switch to an orgasm for him thru penile penetration, then later maybe another orgasm for her by some other route such as the hand or the tongue or maybe even the penis. Though 'addiction" is a possibility I have not yet found an instance of it in my own very extensive practice, which leads me to believe that the danger of such addiction may be exaggerated.

When a woman has learned to bring herself to orgasm, the next step is to invite her lover to observe her doing it. Nothing will instruct him more effectively than the opportunity for this observation. A thousands words cannot be as explicit in helping him understand exactly what she seems to need and when she needs it for orgasmic release. Furthermore, there are no two females alike, so a lesson learned with one woman does not necessarily bestow knowledge of another woman's response pattern.

Some women claim that they would feel highly embarrassed by such a procedure, assuming that their lovers would reject them if they saw such a scene. Usually the reverse is the case. It is an awe inspiring sight to see someone you love developing sexual excitement and releasing it in orgasm. Furthermore, it is the most helpful way I know for two persons to quickly learn each other's needs.

The length of time it takes for a woman to come to orgasm varies from woman to woman. It can happen almost instantly if she is sufficiently readied and if her response mechanism is not blocked. Or it may take upward of an hour or more for an inexperienced woman who has known years of poor conditioning. As I noted earlier, one of the most frustrating things that can happen to the highly sexed but poorly conditioned woman is a great surge of excitement that does not release in orgasm. Such a woman will say "I feel as if I were up against a wall that I can't get through," or "I feel as if I would burst."

If the "wall" breaks, there may result a violently explosive kind of orgasm that is enormously relieving; but if it doesn't the woman may be left in a state of pelvic congestion that is most uncomfortable. Here, especially, women can help themselves by practicing coming to orgasm by the autoerotic route.

Incidentally, autoeroticism has an important place in long-term relationships other than as training experiences for women who are learning to come to orgasm. It offers one solution to the problem of disparity of sexual desire. It can also be very helpful when one partner is sick and the other well, when partners are separated, or when one person is weary and the other 'raring to go'.

The value of allowing feelings to move in a sexual approach can hardly be overestimated. Just as a hand can caress and woo, knowing the full nature of what it touches and conveying the full measure of what the toucher is feeling, or, on the contrary, be nothing more than a machine, so can all sexual contacts be fully responsive and sensitive, or unfortunately, otherwise. One of the most common complaints of lovers is that one or the other is mechanistic in lovemaking.

Awareness of emotional tone, with the courage to respond, requires freeing oneself from one's own fears, along with specific training in how to observe expressions of a partner's moods. (See chapter on love builders.)

Fulfilled sexuality releases creative energy as few other

experiences do. While many persons feel a need for rest and sleep after a satisfying sexual encounter, they usually waken ready to dance right into creative work. The exchange of love energy seems to act for both of them as an inspiration to action, inspiring courage and self confidence.

I have never known either a man or woman who thought of themselves as "bad" at the moment of orgasm. On the contrary, many have described this moment as a time when they have sensed a oneness with God and with the creative principle of life. Perhaps the greatest of the gifts sexuality bestows upon us is this preview of at-one-ness, this merging with God, while we are still encased in bodies of this earth.

Sex is, after all, a way of saying "I love you." The more effectively lovers learn to get this meaning across, the happier their relationships becomes.

10
Relieving Female Sexual Inadequacy

Traditionally, women have had far more problems than men in discovering fullness of joy in sex. Indeed, the legend of the sleeping princess is essentially the story of freeing the woman from a state of sexual frigidity. In the fairy tale, if you remember, the prince, overcoming all obstacles, finally kisses the princess into consciousness (sexual awareness), and they live happily ever after. Many a modern man and woman wish it were that simple.

Today we know that such a "prince" would have had to endow his kisses with something more than determination and passion. He would have had to touch the hidden recesses of the princess's mind, kindling her imagination with the spark of desire; he would have had to rid both her mind and her body of years of bad psychological conditioning; and he would have had to help her replace that conditioning with new reaction patterns that were more conducive to orgastic potential.

The modern princess who suffers from orgasmic inadequacy is more than sleeping. She is literally sexually anesthetized. She is probably emotionally blocked. Her hands and feet are often actually cold. Her body may become rigid and unyielding, when confronted with sex or if it yields at all, it is as an act and not for her own pleasure. Her essential life is lived above the belt, that sacred line of demarcation between the celestial above and the infamous below. She suffers, yet she may not know how deeply she suffers. Like a statue, she may gain a kind of pleasure in being looked at, admired—and *not* touched. But a vacuous pleasure it is indeed!

Fortunately, fewer and fewer of our young women are being led into this disabling state by the wicked "witches" of puritanism who so conscientiously administered the misinformation and emotional malconditioning that resulted in orgasm inadequacy. However, tradition casts a long shadow across the love life of the young. And there are still many modern women who begin their marriages or other committed relationships never having known the ecstasy of completed physical love. Sexual inadequacy in women ranges from the state of almost complete sexual anesthesia, described above, to the bursting frustration of women who are highly aroused but never released through orgasm. Is there anything that can be done to help them in their predicament? Indeed there is.

In terms of treatment it is fairly important to diagnose which of several levels of inadequacy a woman is suffering. In general there are three. The first includes those women who complain that they simply don't feel any thing sexually. They seem to be almost totally anesthetized. The second includes women who experience considerable excitation but cannot release their tension in orgasm. And the third includes women who have had perfectly satisfactory orgastic potency for a period of time in a relationship and then have suddenly lost it and can no longer reach orgasmic release.

With a woman at the "I can't feel" level, first attempts at therapy must be made by helping her feel pleasurable sensations in a generalized way—sight, smell, hearing, but especially touch, with simple sensual pleasure as the goal. Many women in this group suffer severe pleasure anxiety—that is, they perceive any pleasurable sensation as something to be afraid of, and they shut off perception of it and withdraw from the pleasurable stimulus.

Pleasure anxiety is caused early in childhood. The newborn infant experiences all natural bodily functions as pleasurable, of course, but along come the adults in her life, on whom she is dependent for life itself, and these adults express displeasure about everything that gives the baby pleasure, unless they can control or modify these basic physiological acts. If the baby sucks, for example, or defecates or plays with her genitals when she is not intended to, her mother frowns or says, "Naughty baby". So if she is to have what she craves most—approving body contact with Mama—she has to regulate or deny pleasurable functioning in herself. Furthermore, when she has cried for contact, she may have gotten instead the isolation cell treatment—put off in a room by herself to cry it out in her crib. She is helpless to do anything except experience the awful loneliness that follows her attempt to have a pleasurable cuddle. At a much later date when she experiences again the strong longing for body contact with a male, she immediately shuts it off, pretending to herself that she doesn't "want" it. Repeated episodes of the "shut-off" response eventually seal off her ability to perceive or to tolerate intimate bodily pleasure and touch.

In the treatment of such a woman it would be useless to encourage genitality at once. First her mind has to be won to the idea that she is really missing something of value. She has to begin to want to open herself to pleasurable touch sensations instead of rejecting them.

Literally, she must become as a little child and learn from the beginning how delightful is all manner of affectional touch. She must learn to let her partner "pleasure" her body all over without making any demand on her for specific genital response. He must stay away from touch contact with her lower pelvic area and from her breasts and begin by stroking her back, caressing her face, rubbing her legs, and so forth. Gradually, as she "comes alive", she should begin to "pleasure" herself genitally with her own hands. I have already talked about the value of learning to masturbate and of the use of the vibrator as an "assist" if orgastic response is deeply blocked.

Just as soon as such a woman begins to gain some confidence that pleasure is a positive gain and not a signal for disaster, it is time for her to invite her partner to help her come to orgasm by the manual route.

At this point the treatment of the almost totally anesthetized woman (no longer so anesthetized) is somewhat similar to that of the woman who is able to become aroused but doesn't release her tension in orgasm.

Related to this and particularly pertinent to orgasm potential, women have a special problem which is not generally recognized. This has to do with the relationship of sexual mobility to the ability to discharge anger tensions. Let me explain.

If we accept the premise that emotion, by definition, is "feeling in movement", we shortly observe that the movement of certain feelings involves specific musculature. For example, an angry person wants to let his or her body move aggressively. Muscles tense for action—namely, those muscles involved in hitting, scratching, kicking, biting, pounding, and screaming. If tension is not discharged physically through some substitute but similar movement, the result is a tightening of these muscles. Boy children are expected to draft off anger tensions through aggressive sports or even through aggressive action, but girl children are never expected to get angry in the first place and certainly not show it. "Nice little girls don't get angry" is

Relieving Female Sexual Inadequacy

what is hurled at the girl child as she grows up. Yet she is just as prone to feelings of irritation and anger as is her brother. So what does she do but tighten the muscles that control the movements we recognize as aggressive anger; and she also breathes more shallowly. Furthermore, she rarely relaxes these muscles fully, and so they tend to remain chronically tight.

All this would not be so serious except for the fact that it is impossible for sexual feeling to move through the muscular blockade of held-onto anger. When the large muscles that control hitting, kicking, pounding, are in a state of chronic contraction, they will not permit the soft flow of tender feeling to move easily, if at all. This cuts off genital feeling and tends to result in the problem that so many women face, that of being sexually aroused and yet unable to relieve sexual tension through orgasm. They come up against the familiar "wall" through which they cannot move. Further, the more excited they become without release, the more distressed. There is no use in working on more and better techniques of stimulation for such a woman. The first job is to teach her to discharge anger tensions in physical terms. Beat a couch, pound a pillow, scream, bang pots and pans around. All of these are useful discharge mechanisms. They hurt no one, and they relieve the tension that the woman is holding onto for dear life, indeed, for fear that if she really let go, she might jolly well kill someone.

I suggest to my own female patients that they lie flat on their backs on a bed and then pretend that they are two-year-old children having tantrums, kick legs up and down, bang fists on the mattress, and yell. Most people feel pretty silly the first time they do this, but almost invariably they acknowledge the relief that follows immediately. Also, they begin to breathe as they have never breathed before, their exhalations bringing sheer pleasure.

Most women are terribly frightened of their own anger,

largely because they don't know what will happen if it is released. It is as if the world might fall apart. The unfortunate truth is that when such women *did* express anger as small children, they *were* punished for it. Now they are defended against even feeling anger, and the defense has, in turn, created a muscular block against the free flow of sexual feeling.

The emotion of sorrow is more acceptable to women, though it becomes something of a problem to men. Many a woman releases not only her sadness but her anger by the route of tears, and many a man, distressed by tears, will say, "There, there, dear, don't cry, don't cry". What a woman needs at this point is just the reverse. She needs a man who can say, "Come, have a good cry on my shoulder, dear; it will make you feel better". This helps her to release the tension of pent-up sadness and opens her whole organism to a freer flow of sexual-love energy. In other words, it not only makes sexuality more accessible, but allows sexual energy to proceed through to orgasm without muscular impediment.

What so frequently happens to women who can't release sexual tension in orgasm is that their entire pelvic musculature has become as hard and unyielding as a rock. Then it has them in a grip of steel, through which the streaming, rippling sensations that would carry them through to orgasm simply cannot move. These women must learn how to unlock such spasms—and will be able to as they learn to breathe.

A woman who is having difficulty responding to a hesitant husband is often sexually electrified by contact with another man who is handling himself with strength and authority in his sexual expressiveness. If and when her husband begins to move with greater sexual authority, she is more responsive to him also.

In some recess of her being she senses his strength and by

contagion acquires some of his confidence for herself. With such a man she is freed to let herself go, for she knows that he not only can take care of himself, but will have energy to spare for taking care of her.

The opposite of this desirable kind of attention is expressed in the story of a woman who complained of taking so long to come to orgasm because her partner watched television while playing with her genitals in his half-hearted attempts to bring her to orgasm.

The woman who has once been orgastic and then ceases to be is almost always a woman who has fallen out of love with her mate, or she may have lost respect for him or feel that he is not the man she expected him to be.

Quite often another man has come into her life as well, and suffering from the notion that a woman is not allowed to love more than one man at a time, she becomes nonorgasmic with her partner.

She needs to have a talk with a therapist who will encourage her to give voice to her feelings and who can, perhaps, help her bring these feelings into proper focus. Perhaps, with the aid of therapy she can again share a satisfying sexual relationship with her partner. Or perhaps she needs to be told that many women can joyously love two men. Or perhaps she may need to come to terms with a fact that she may fully love another woman more than the male partner she has united her life with.

Occasionally a woman will complain: "I get excited sexually. I feel that I want sexual intercourse; but when my partner tries to penetrate, my vagina contracts involuntarily and I pull away and he cannot get in. Is there any thing I can do about this?"

This is called vaginismus. It is the involuntary contraction of the muscles in the outer third of the vagina, and the contraction is generally so strong that it can prevent penile penetration.

The sex histories of such women usually contain some sexually frightening experience such as attempted rape, violation by a trusted male, or even the shocking interruption of a childhood masturbatory act. The treatment generally requires psychotherapy directed toward understanding the nature of the condition and its emotional orgins, along with specific training in learning to relax the vaginal muscles. Again, exercises aimed at teaching a woman to relax all the muscles in her pelvis, her anus, and her urethra are of help.

Hypnosis can sometimes be helpful but should be administered only by a competent therapist. After the causative factors are understood, the therapist may teach the woman to self-induce hypnosis as a relaxative technique. She then suggests to herself that she is about to enjoy a sensuously pleasurable experience and that the muscles of her vagina are indeed opening up to receive the penis that will bring her this delightful sensation. She may find that her involuntary contraction reverses to a relaxed state of receptivity.

Women can be taught to contract and relax their vaginas on a voluntary basis. This helps to establish muscle tone as well as is useful in the treatment of vaginismus. In the treatment of vaginismus, however, the emphasis must be on the *release* rather than on the contraction. It is very helpful to insert a finger, contract upon it voluntarily, then equally voluntarily try to relax the muscles that have contracted. Many physicians give the woman a series of graduated dilators to practice inserting. Personally, I have found that the coldness and hardness of these have militated against the "opening-up" process. A warm well-lubricated finger—the woman's own or better yet, her lover's which she gently guides, always controlling the depth of the insertion—can gradually "teach" the vaginal muscles a new way of behaving.

It cannot be emphasized often enough that the body is very responsive to the imaginative processes of the mind. The vaginal muscles cannot be "willed" to open and relax, but they may well open and relax of themselves when *imagination* is joined with specific training of vaginal muscles.

The sharp focus of attention on images of delicious sensation connected with *opening* and *receiving* are most useful; for example, visual images in the mind's eye of opening flowers, outstretched arms, opening lips. Also, practice in the art of becoming open and receptive in noncoital situations has some carry-over effect in coital ones. For example, simply learning to listen to others with palms open and up, rather than with fists clenched, can make a difference in how one hears people, and in turn it can make a difference in how one receives a man coitally. Learning to empathize will help one recognize whom and what one can trust, and since trusting is an essential part of permitting oneself to open vaginally, a woman will find that empathy gives a more valid basis for the degree of trust she needs.

Masters and Johnson have found that when vaginismus is present, there is also a high degree of impotence in the male partner. Which came first is sometimes hard to determine. However, they found that the four most usual causes of vaginismus are (1) impotence or premature ejaculation in the male partner, (2) rigid emotional control, as in religious orthodoxy, (3) specific sexually traumatic episodes in earlier life, and (4) attempted sex with a man by a woman who was primarily homosexual.

The treatment used most successfully by this famous team of clinician-researchers has been to demonstrate to both man and woman under medical supervision and in the doctor's examining room that there was an actual involuntary constriction of the muscles of the outer third of the vagina whenever there was any attempt to insert anything. Then when both partners had recognized the involuntary nature of the contraction, they were given a series of graduated dilators which the man, under his partner's guidance and control, practiced inserting into her vagina in the privacy of their own bedroom. The co-therapists also recommended to their patients that when they were able to insert one of the larger of these dilators, it should be left in the vagina for a few hours, simply to accustom the vaginal muscles to the "feel" of containment. Masters and Johnson were able to cure all their patients of vaginismus within three to five days if they had the full and intensive cooperation of both husband and wife. This is a remarkable record when one considers that many therapists have taken months and months to achieve the same ends by utilizing verbal techniques alone, and even then many have not succeeded in helping their patients at all.

There is a real problem of timing for many women but especially for the woman who is coupled with a man who suffers from premature ejaculation. Instead of being able to focus on her own growing sexual excitation, she worries about how fast he will come, thus leaving her high and unsatisfied, and this distraction in itself sends her back down the excitement scale. After a number of episodes of this kind, she is likely to become one of those women who feel "used", unless he is thoughtful enough to bring her to orgasm by the manual route if he has arrived at climax too fast for her to "catch up."

Even when a man is not a premature ejaculator, there are numerous women who take such a long time to come to orgasm that rare would be the man who could maintain an erection long enough to satisfy them. And there are other women who can never come to climax except with such manual or oral stimulation of the clitoral area. A man who values his partner's fulfillment might well be prepared then to bring her to orgasm in these ways, either previous to or following his own coming to climax. When she is relieved of the fear of not coming to orgasm herself, she may well go on to a second orgasm with her lover's penis inside her, and her second orgasm sometimes occurs simultaneously with his release.

Such a technique also has the advantage of freeing a woman to concentrate on her own sensations of pleasure for a brief moment of time. Men have always been free to do this, but women have been conditioned to believe that they must see to it that the man is satisfied. The focus on the "other" at this particular moment is not conducive to quickening or intensifying one's own sexual excitation. So when a man is undemanding for himself until his partner is satisfied, he frees her to concentrate on her own sensation and fantasies; then when she comes to orgasm, she finds herself wanting to do the same for him.

Sometimes a woman's mind drifts off over numerous nonsexual matters during an episode of manual stimulation. When this occurs, she drops down the sexual excitement scale, sometimes prolonging the lovemaking to the point of real fatigue for the man. Or she may "worry" that he is bored or tired with the process—or that the children need her or that the telephone is about to ring, etc., etc.—and that she will then have to respond to such "fire calls" and thus interrupt her sexual pleasure.

This is the time when she must learn to discipline herself to put all nonsexual thoughts aside, to shut them out of the bedroom and lock the door of her mind to them. Her lover can help by verbally directing her thoughts to her own sexual sensations. He can also be alert to what seems to be pleasing her physically and can then continue that pattern of stimulation without change. The latter is important. Many a man, thinking that his partner may be tiring of one sort of caressing, starts another—of a different pattern.

More likely than not, the change itself will drop a woman down, rather than up, the excitement scale, and often she will have to build again a whole new set of fantasy thoughts and feelings around the new stimulus, which takes additional time and may even discourage them both. When a woman discovers her lover doing something that is "working" for her she should tell him to keep right on doing what he is doing. If his caressing is not exactly what gives pleasure, she should show him how to better it in line with her own desires. The most effective thing in the world here is for her to guide his hand or invite him to watch her use her own hand for a few moments, until he gets the hang of what is stimulating to her.

One female complaint that the sex therapists often hear is the following: "The entrance to my vagina feels so irritated that when we have intercourse, I can hardly stand it. I've been to the doctor, and he says it's just a mild fungus infection. He treats it, and after a few days it seems all right for a few weeks, but then it comes back again and again. I'm embarrassed to go to him anymore, but I just can't stand intercourse because it's so irritating".

Unfortunately, doctors are far too cavalier in their treatment of fungus infections. The treatment can indeed be long and tedious, requiring cooperation on the part of both partners as well as the doctor.

It is also true that for adequate results, the man may have to receive treatment simultaneously with his wife, or he will reinfect her, even though he himself does not suffer from the infection. He must also refrain from contact with any other woman unless he wears a condom, and, of course, he must wear a condom when he has intercourse with his wife until she is completely free from the infection. Furthermore, a woman should be checked by her doctor regularly for a period of at least three months to make certain that the infection remains cleared. Fungus infections are worth clearing up, for they can interfere tremendously with sexual pleasure.

Dyspareunia is a medical term meaning painful intercourse. There are many reasons for this problem, most of which require diagnosis and treatment by a well-trained gynecologist. Certainly, if a woman suffers pain during coition, she should consult her doctor, and before her doctor tells her that the pain is all in her head, she should find out if he is acquainted with new findings in sex research.

Certainly, every effort to bring a woman to orgastic ability is worth making. For a woman to function at her best, she needs orgasm. Furthermore, such a woman can give her children emotional support in their own sex development.

11
Relieving Male Sexual Inadequacy

Human males, being human, are susceptible to inadequacy in their sexual lives, just as they are in other areas of living. Somehow, however, these inadequacies seem to carry a special onus because of the silly social expectation that anyone can do "what comes naturally." For example, inexperienced women assume that all men are impassioned Lotharios, given the chance; but many a woman has discovered that her young lover was as shy as a virgin and quite incapable of an erection on their initial attempt at sexual lovemaking. If the matter stopped there, they could both forget it, charging it off to factors such as fatigue or nervousness. But sex fear, for him, may have taken over, and his temporary impotence may persist.

Then all too often a woman makes a series of critical mistakes that can be quite damaging. Generally, she starts out by erroneously assuming that *she* must be unattractive, unappealing, and unloved—hence her lover's impotence. When that seems improbable, she suspects that he may have another woman on the string. She may even accuse him of it. Even after she has assured herself that she was wrong here, too, she may start imagining the possibility of homosexuality or that something is medically wrong with him.

He may tell her that his work is exhausting, and she may believe him until she finds him perfectly capable of playing eighteen holes of golf on a Saturday afternoon, though much too tired for sex. Sooner or later they may have enough sense to consult a sex therapist, but by then a lot of damage has been done, and it would have been far better for both of them had they known enough to recognize sex fear when confronted with it.

Although it may be true that considerably fewer manifestations of sexual anxiety exist in men than in woman, their existence in the former are of sufficient frequency and severity to deeply upset many loving and committed relationships. Men have grown up in the same kind of sex-negative families as women, and for many men these were almost as repressive in their effect as they were for women. It is small wonder, then, that some of the negativity washed off on them, especially on those who suffered unusual sex shock.

During courtship such fears rarely reveal themselves. A young man can unconsciously hide behind the folklore that "protects" the unmarried girl from the male's "animal passions". He "respects" her virginity, even when she is not particularly desirous of this kind of protection and "respect," and probably is not even a virgin.

During this period he has petted and caressed and indulged in all manner of noncoital techniques within the limits of technical virginity. He has certainly had erections that convince both himself and his beloved that once they are living together—either in marriage or in some other committed relationship acceptable to them both, they will be able to indulge the passions so excitingly and mutually aroused.

Unintentionally, he has deceived not only his lover but himself, for he does not consciously acknowledge that he suffers sexual anxiety. Only when the time actually arrives for him to prove his manhood does he make the startling discovery that he cannot. This is a critical moment for any two lovers.

If she treats this initial failure casually and tenderly, emphasizing his ability to arouse and satisfy her with noncoital lovemaking, he may be able to overcome his anxiety in very short order. But if she acts as if the sky has fallen in, he may become so despairing that he will need sensitive professional assistance to reestablish confidence.

When early failure occurs, the patience and understanding of the woman will be as important to the man's early recovery as similar qualities are to an anxious virgin, if the tables are reversed.

Erectile ability is entirely natural, as natural as breathing. No man needs to be taught how—in fact, he cannot be taught how. Nor can any man get an erection by willing it. Erection is a completely involuntary act which occurs when a man experiences adequate pleasurable stimuli, either from within or from without.

Impotence is largely psychogenic in nature—that is to say, it is almost always a psychological, rather than a medical, problem. A rough rule of thumb differentiating medical from psychological causation is the following: If a man sometimes awakens in the morning with an erection, he can usually assume that his impotence in intercourse is of emotional origin. He will need a sex therapist, not a physician. Better yet, he will need a nondemanding sex partner who can focus his attention on sensual pleasure and dissipate his feeling that he must "perform".

The roots of impotence frequently lie in childhood, mostly in fear-provoking interruptions of early masturbation or in the mother's negative treatment of the infant son's sexual organs or of his early sexual activity.

In spite of such negative experiences, however, the sexual urge is so strong that given positive encouragement and understanding, along with new conditioning, the majority of men can regain potency.

Some religions have thoroughly reinforced the myth that there are two kinds of women—the virgins whom men marry and the girls of the street, with whom they have sex but do not marry. With the former, boys are not permitted to so much as nurture a sexual thought, let alone act. The latter they can take to bed at will with very little twinge of conscience. This is now a very old-fashioned concept.

However, a man so indoctrinated may get along well in his sexual activities with the Mary Magdalenes, but when he gets his supposedly virgin, "Mary," the conditioning of the "good girl" taboo takes over. Willy-nilly he can't perform, to his great chagrin.

One of the pesty problems with impotence is the reinforcing effect of a "failure". A man fears that because he has "failed once", he will do so again. From the moment fear enters the picture, it stimulates further failure, and the man is enmeshed in a vicious circle. He begins to believe that he cannot or that there is something critically wrong with him that can't be cured.

He may then retreat into work, inviting its absorption to the point of exhaustion, or he may spend more nights with other men than he really enjoys; or he may initiate a frenzied social life with his partner that wearies them both; or if he is wise, he and his partner may see a sex therapist.

Generally, impotence may be cured by treatment that (1) helps a man understand the roots of his problem, (2) dissipates his fears, and (3) focuses his attention on sensual pleasure instead of on performance.

There is nothing quite so effective as a woman who is delighted—nay, charmed—with her lover's sexual organs as well as by his other attributes.

One especially effective remedy that a wife can initiate on

her own is to pet and pay attention to his penis at a time and place that they both know would be impossible for him to respond coitally. Since it is obviously impossible to have intercourse at that moment, the man can relax and enjoy the stimulation. He knows that he cannot be asked to take responsibility in a moving car, for example, and so he loses his anxiety about having something expected of him that he can't deliver. Usually he will get an erection and enjoy it, thus proving to himself that he is not impotent after all. With confidence rebuilt he may gradually come to enjoy intercourse at a later time, especially if no pressure is put on him for performance.

If women could only be taught to accept wholeheartedly the beauty of male sexual anatomy, it would go a long way in preventing the problem of male impotence. So many men have been taught to believe that their penis is unattractive to women, just as women have been brainwashed to believe that their own sexual structures are unbeautiful to men. When a woman looks admiringly at her husband's genitalia and gets across to him her utter delight in the movement of the penis, its texture, its fragrance, he begins to build more confidence in his ability to please her, and very frequently his impotence quite magically disappears.

When a man shows signs of impotence, the most helpful thing to do is to return at once to the old petting techniques that proved mutually arousing during courtship. Forget trying to have intercourse at all, and concentrate instead on giving each other delightful allover bodily sensations, eventually bringing each other to orgasm by noncoital means. Gradually, the pleasureable association of stimulation, arousal, erection, release, become part of usually-to-be-expected behavior, offsetting fear of failure.

Frequent causes of impotence, other than fear, are alcohol, fatigue, and anxiety in general. It is said that one drink may loosen inhibitions but that several drinks lessen a man's capacity for erection. It is well for both man and woman to remember that when they hope to enjoy sex after a night's entertainment on the town. Of course, this varies and there are those who enjoy some relaxation of this sort before coitus.

I have already discussed the temporary impotence that sometimes occurs with men who are under stress in business or professional life. This clears of itself when the stress is removed unless a man starts to worry about it.

There are, of course, medical reasons for some forms of impotence. These are relatively rare, and most men suffering impotence for any length of time have already checked the possibility of medical causation with their physicians. (It is much easier for people to accept medical causative reasons for sexual inadequacy than emotional ones, and so they generally go first to their doctor for advice and consultation.) A word of caution is in order. It is unforgivable, but true, that some medical authorities have imposed searing trauma on male sufferers that is completely unnecessary and unjustified. Such physicians, finding no medical reason for impotence, indicate to the patient that he must simply learn to live with his disability—that there is no hope of cure or relief.

Since men are enormously suggestible in the area of sex, the edict of authority reinforces what many men fear anyway. Obviously, such a doctor is unacquainted with current findings and current psychophysiological methods of treatment.

Even worse are the religious "authorities" acting as counselors who indicate to a male sufferer that his impotence is due to moral straying from the path of righteousness or due to the normal act of masturbation. Both suggestions are utter nonsense, but some men believe these crippling myths just because someone in authority has spoken. Then, of course, impotence worsens.

Let me say again, most impotence responds to treatment, and the best treatment is freedom from fear and relearning how to enjoy pleasurable sensual as well as sexual sensations at the hands of an appreciative and nondemanding person.

Another form of male sexual inadequacy is premature ejaculation, which is really just another form of scared sexual response, learned early and carried into adult life. It often stems from that kind of childhood conditioning that has forced a boy to learn to masturbate quickly so as to avoid parental discovery. Later, as an adult, when faced with the enchanting prospect of sanctioned sex with a beloved woman, he "comes" too fast—sometimes so fast that he cannot even effect penetration.

His lover may complain, "He comes to climax so quickly that I never have a chance to feel anything, let alone come to climax myself. Is there anything we can do about this?"

Indeed there is. In fact, there are several techniques that have brought successful results, and with cooperation from a willing woman nearly every man who suffers from premature ejaculation can change this pattern of response.

Dr. James H. Seman has devised one simple technique for such reconditioning.* After obtaining the cooperation of both man and woman, he instructs the woman to caress her lover's penis with her hands. When he gets the signal that he is about to ejaculate he tells her to stop, allowing him to rest before continuing again. Such practice sessions at home are carried on until the time interval for the man's need to ejaculate coincides approximately with his partner's time requirement for coming to orgasm. Next Dr. Semans instructs the woman to introduce a lubricant upon her hands (for example, cold cream), which simulates the lubricated internal environment of the vagina. Again, prac-

---

*"Premature Ejaculation: A New Approach," *Southern Medical Journal*, 49, no. 1 (April, 1956): 353–58.

tice sessions are carried on until the signal for ejaculation arrives after longer and longer sex play. When he can control his need to ejaculate in the lubricated hand of his partner, he is usually ready to do so intravaginally.

There is one element in Dr. Semans's method that particularly recommends itself to me. The very fact that the woman supportively approves her lover's penis, looks at it, handles it with tenderness and love, coaxing it into greater pleasure, provides the man with the necessary *yes* to his own hesitant sexuality, counteracting the puritanical crippling *so* inflicted on him as a child and which probably accounted for his problem in the first place.

Dr. William Masters, of the Masters and Johnson team of sex researchers, has worked out a somewhat different technique that the team has found highly successful.*

Again, the cooperation of both man and wife is required. The woman semireclines against pillows with her legs spread wide. The man settles down between them, lying flat on the bed, his head toward the foot of it. His knees are flexed, and his legs straddle her hips. This gives the woman complete free range with her hands to pleasure the man's genitals at will. She then strokes and caresses his penis until he gets a signal that he is about to ejaculate, at which moment he instructs her to squeeze the end of the penis for three to four seconds and then immediately release it for fifteen to thirty seconds before continuing caressing. In mastering the "squeeze technique" she should use her thumb on one side of the coronal ridge and her first and second fingers on the other side, the first finger being above the ridge and the second finger below it. Her partner can show her how hard to squeeze so as not to hurt him, but a fairly strong degree of pressure is required.

The sex research team responsible for this technique

*William Masters and Virginia Johnson, *Human Sexual Inadequacy* (Boston: Little, Brown and Company, 1970), pp. 101–15.

finds that the "stimulation-squeeze" combination can readily teach a man to contain ejaculation for periods of fifteen to twenty minutes within a couple of days. When this has been accomplished, they suggest that the woman mount the man for direct coital contact, but they instruct her to kneel over him (with knees at about the level of his navel, from which position she is able to move back on, rather than sit down on, the shaft of his penis, and she is to remain very still, allowing the man to move only enough to maintain his erection). If ejaculation threatens to occur, she is in a position to readily withdraw long enough to apply the squeeze technique, and when the impulse is dissipated, to again return to her coital position. Gradually, when they have had several practice sessions in which the man has successfully managed erection without ejaculation, they can begin to move more freely. Always, when ejaculation seems imminent, she can withdraw and "squeeze," which regularly brings his ejaculatory urge under control.

Finally, the couple is encouraged to transfer their coital position from that of the woman above, man below position to the lateral coital position.

Apparently the value of this position lies in the utter freedom of movement that it gives both man and woman and the freedom from tension that it provides the man. The position that is generally considered most popular in the United States—namely the man above, woman below—is not very helpful for a man who has suffered from premature ejaculation, since it presents the greatest difficulties for ejaculatory control.

Masters and Johnson emphasize the need for precoital play. They also carefully warn their patients to continue practice sessions for at least a year after their intensive treatment period, since they have found that it takes about that time to firmly establish new learning patterns. In addition they caution their patients not to be alarmed if the man experiences a brief period of impotence. This is the result of exhaustion, and nothing more. In their newfound joy in coital activity many couples will overdo it for a while. The suggestion is simply to take it a bit easier and to return to the practice sessions whenever the problem of prematurity returns.

This technique has served to increase the sexual excitement and pleasure of the woman as well as retrain the man to bring his ejaculatory response under his own control. For their careful work and explicit directions we have much to be thankful for from the research team in St. Louis.

I teach all my own patients one additional thing—how to breathe so as to send a pleasurable, streaming sensation down into the genital region as they exhale. Many of my patients have a great deal of difficulty at first in tolerating the pure pleasure involved. This is what psychologists call pleasure anxiety. But as they learn to better their breathing techniques and to handle the resulting pleasure, they report vastly improved sexual response and control.

From the discussion above it must be obvious by now that if a man suffers sexual inadequacy for any appreciable time, both partners should consult a competent sex therapist. Avoid all recrimination, and try to put away all fears and fantasies that interfere with the free-flowing quality of love. Sexual inadequacy is amenable to treatment.

12
Pregnancy: Planned and Unplanned

Many of you are looking forward with keen anticipation to having your first baby. The adventure of giving birth to a living, breathing, tangible evidence of your union leaves you feeling as close to God as man and woman can get.

Babies are no longer a duty or an obligation in a world suffering from a population explosion. They are a privilege and a reward. They are, presumably, the *raison d'etre* for the legal framework of marriage; and marriage is, among other things, a contract for the protection of children. Most of you probably assumed that you would have children when you married, but because of this tacit assumption, some of you may have neglected to discuss it until after marriage.

More often than I like to remember, a saddened young woman or man enters my office, deeply grieved and bewildered because his or her mate refuses to have a child. Alternatively, one or the other insists on too many children—sometimes too many for the strength and ability of the complainant to handle without undue strain.

Every man or woman who is capable of warming a child's life with love deserves the chance to do so, and it is nothing short of tragic for that person when the gate is closed. Not that one cannot find compensatory things to do in life, but

Pregnancy: Planned and Unplanned

there really is no adequate compensation for childlessness to someone who longs to hold a baby or to take responsibility for a child.

Although most normal, healthy people want children and expect to have them, there are any number of experiences that a person can go through in the process of growing up that create fear tensions, with resultant refusal to have a child. Sometimes girls have acquired impressions of terror connected with childbearing. Such girls need professional help to erase these impressions and to implant healthy ones. Sometimes men harbor the most desolate memories connected with babies, infancy, and helplessness. Such men also need professional help. Sometimes a young person's professional career captures his or her time and energy so fully that he or she fails to grant to the other the fulfillment of the parental role for fear that it will interfere with that career.

These are rather negative things to be drawing to your attention, but I do so to indicate the real need for two young people to communicate to each other their feelings about having children. And not only about having them, but about their philosophy of caring for them (though I must hastily add that when people are confronted by flesh and blood babies of their own, their notions about child rearing change significantly, thank heavens). I do want to note, in all fairness, that many a young man or woman resists the idea of children at first, yet later becomes a devoted parent.

If you sense that there is a deep resistance on the part of your husband (or wife) to having a child, while you confidently expect to raise a family, or if this is a subject that neither of you has talked about, it is high time to raise the issue of the importance of these hopes and dreams to you. If you run into a snag that the two of you cannot resolve, this is a good time to see a marriage counselor. The matter of wanting or not wanting children is basic, and disagreement which is not resolved can destroy even the most loving of partnerships.

Here are some clues that may be helpful:

1. It may be that your partner (and this can be either the man or the woman) has not had enough chance to be central in his (or her) life. He (or she) needs to "be the baby" for a bit and is frightened that the love of the partner will be drained away from him (or her) if a real baby enters the scene.

Actually, most of us do need more babying than we have had. Some of us have been so deprived of the early and primary forms of mothering that we are left with exceptional hungers. Here again is the principle of "the half-filled cup that cannot runneth over." The two of you, knowing this, can deliberately set out to do something about it. Even at this late date, a wife can provide her husband with the kind of emotional fulfillment that permits him to grow up, freeing him from the clinging need to *be* the baby. A husband can do the same for his wife. I have seen some imaginative experiments along this line carried out by devoted lovers, with remarkable results.

It is one of the good reasons, of course, for planning a period of marriage without children. This hiatus provides a couple with the chance to give to each other the many indulgences that each may need before either is ready to take on responsibility for a child.

2. It may be that babies have been associated with duty, deprivation, unwanted tasks, unenjoyable sensory experences—like being made to change the baby's diapers when you were young and hating it—or staying in from playing ball with the gang to baby-sit while mother did her other chores.

Such an adult needs to learn that these reactions are the result of unhappy conditioning in youth and that a man and his wife can create an altogether different situation. True, babies do impose certain tasks upon those who care for them, but these can be so managed that they are experienced as pleasurable, not odious. It may help to expose yourself to some family where things are done differently; where the baby isn't always howling, making messes, taking mother away from father, but is, instead, a contented little being with a mother and father who go about their accustomed lives with the minimum of discombobulation and the maximum of fulfillment of everyone's needs, including the baby's. I knew one wise wife who borrowed a cute, responsive toddler for short periods on weekends. Her husband fell in love with the child and wanted to "start a baby" right away. Sometimes the husband or wife has had no experience at all with a baby and just dreads the unknown or doubts his or her capacity to cope with it.

3. Sometimes a woman has invested a lot of herself in preparing for her professional life and she cannot bear the thought of interrupting this while taking time out for babies. Or a husband feels that his professional needs will give way before the child's demands. Often this is only a temporary state of affairs, and there is much to be said for young people getting their two feet firmly on the ground before starting a family. But it becomes a different matter if year after year goes by and one postpones agreement to have a baby while the other keeps yearning for one.

If the woman is hesitant, perhaps she and her husband can figure out a way for her to "have her cake and eat it too." With careful management, it is quite possible to have a baby and continue working. Thousands of women do. It may require fuller cooperation on the part of her husband, but if it is he who is pressing for a child, he may be more than willing to share the care of that child (to the youngster's great advantage, I might add, since children need the attention of fathers as well as of mothers).

If the husband is the hesitant one, a wise wife may be able to show him that she can manage their home and their children with minimum inconvenience to his professional commitments.

Economic considerations play a considerable role in the mutual decision of every couple as to when to start their family. However, most parents will tell you that there is never a time when a young couple can afford a baby—they just plunge in and somehow swim for the far shore. Most parents make it. One family I know says it's like getting on a roller coaster. Certainly, it is your right, however, to decide on a time that seems to be most convenient to your *total* plan. Most partners in love look forward to that time eagerly.

In general, if you can have your "druthers," baby-having is best postponed until both of you have completed your education and until at least one of you has a job that can provide you with food, clothing, and a roof over your heads, plus medical insurance. The frills can wait.

I am often quite surprised by couples who feel they cannot afford a baby yet manage to support a car, a TV set, and a number of unnecessary gadgets. One simply has to conclude that their values are a bit twisted or that they don't really want children after all.

Having a baby does cost something, and that something needs to be planned for. Most people have to figure around a thousand dollars, which covers obstetric fees, the hospital, and the initial supplies needed for the baby. Medical insurance helps a lot, and if you are lucky enough to be included in a group that has a maternity coverage, you hardly have to worry about the additional economic burden.

A bigger problem may be the loss of the mother's earnings to the family income. However, if you plan for this from the very beginning and save part of her salary, if possible, or base your standard of living on what the husband can earn, rather than on your combined earnings, you will have little to fear about meeting your economic responsibilites.

Many a young couple has succeeded in continuing at their jobs *and* taking care of a baby, by a careful husbandry of time and energy and by sharing the baby care and housework. It is not as impossible or unpleasant as one might suppose.

The trick is to keep things simple. Fancy nurseries and multiple gadgets compound both work and cost. All a baby really needs is the warmth and comfort of a mother's arms, milk from her giving breasts, a pile of diapers, some nightgowns and blankets, a few bottles, and a basket to sleep in close to the mother and daddy. (Yes, I know that this is heresy. But the most secure babies in the world are brought through infancy thus.) The rest is all frosting. Anyone in America can afford these essentials. As a baby grows up, so do the parents and their income. Little by little, they stretch to meet the demands of their growing family. Perhaps this is one of the reasons why people with children amount to more in their businesses and professions and in society than those without children. Parents *have* to stretch to fill the needs of children, and they end up by becoming bigger persons themselves.

Where and how in your community can you get help with family planning? Any couple may seek such assistance from a Planned Parenthood Clinic. Or you may ask your local hospital for the names of several reputable gynecologists or obstetricians from whom you may seek contraceptive advice. When you phone for your appointment, tell him or her the purpose of your visit. Since a few physicians will not provide birth control information because of their religious convictions, this gives the doctor a chance to tell you so and avoid the inconvenience of a fruitless visit. If you run into this difficulty with one, simply try another. Most doctors will readily help you if their training has included this specialty.

The way a pregnancy proceeds depends a great deal on the kind of education a couple can get to prepare them for it. Such education is left out of most of our secondary schools and colleges. This is pure idiocy, for the rearing of children is one of the biggest, most important jobs that any couple can tackle, requiring skill and knowledge. What is the sense of studying biology, yet leaving out training for childbirth and child rearing?

Fortunately, there are some social institutions which

provide *adults* with such education, at least in our large cities. The Visiting Nurse Association has pioneered many such courses. The Maternity Center Association of New York City (48 East 92nd Street, New York, New York) offers free courses to couples expecting a child. What is more, they keep in touch with similar attempts around the country so that a postcard sent to them may bring you information as to courses in your neighborhood.

The "Natural Childbirth Movement," promulgated by parents and physicians who are concerned with creating an environment for birth that is conducive to family unity and happiness, has many branches in various parts of the country. In Seattle, Washington, one of the best of these programs has been offered by The Association for Childbirth Education (located in the Y.W.C.A. on Seneca Street).

Perhaps, if you simply call your local hospital and ask for the names of its obstetricians who use natural childbirth techniques, you will locate some good resources. Because this method requires education, the doctors who use it may have devised a training program in which you can enroll.

Sometimes, young couples ask me what effect a *premarital* pregnancy will have upon their marriage. Will they feel resentful of each other in later years?

They needn't—and they don't if they were planning to marry anyway. Difficulties come when a couple marries *solely* because the girl is pregnant and not because they love each other. I would not recommend a loveless marriage on any account. Both man and woman are better off if they act in some responsible way in respect to the coming child, yet do not consummate the marriage.

A girl who wants to keep her baby can do so if she manages to keep her wits about her and if she has considerable personal strength. In today's world many women choose not to marry and yet do wish to raise a child—so many, in fact, that the fatherless child is no longer looked at askance at least in many parts of the country.

The chances are that the mother will shortly marry someone she truly loves, thus making it possible for the baby to grow up in a *happy* family unit.

If she feels that she cannot keep the baby, there are adoptive families waiting for almost every infant that is available for adoption. She should let an adoptive agency know that she is willing to give her child up, and they will help her with the details.

Either of the above plans is, in my opinion, better than marrying a person you do not love.

Let's go back to the couple in love who get caught in a pregnancy before they celebrate their marriage.

Lots of young people are just as delighted with their premarital pregnancies as older married couples are with theirs. I know for certain that at least some premarital pregnancies are as close to "planned" as they can be. These are sometimes used as levers to persuade elders that the young are ready for marriage. (Rather ridiculous, of course, because the biggest evidence one could give of *not* being ready would be to need a lever of this sort.)

Most premarital pregnancies are sheer accident, and sometimes rather inconvenient accidents at that. They often make necessary a sudden and drastic shift in plans, including a hasty marriage with all that this may include. These adjustments call for maturity and real strength of character on the part of young people.

It means that the young husband must recognize that the total personality of his wife may change from that of the non-pregnant girl he fell in love with. This may bewilder him, making him wonder if marriage was what changed her. Certainly, it will take patience and understanding on his part to realize that "this too shall pass" and that some months after the baby is born he will recover the girl he thought he knew before their marriage. He would have had a sounder realization of this had he had a chance to live with her in the non-pregnant state for a while first; and patience would have been easier to muster.

A man's personality may also seem to change during his wife's pregnancy. In his anxiety about whether he can meet the test of manhood imposed by the support of new and dependent life, he may forget some of the niceties that he showered upon his fiancée during courtship, and this may not be easy for his bride to bear.

However, young couples *do* manage to weather all the changes in personality imposed on both man and wife by a pregnancy. On the whole, they manage well. It is easier if they choose their associates from among other young couples who are also having babies and if they enroll together in a course preparing them for their new status.

What, then, are some of these personality changes in the woman likely to be? What is the emotional life of a woman like during pregnancy?

To begin with, she experiences many sensations that are new to her. She finds it necessary, at times, to get used to a body that behaves differently. Some of the feelings may be perceived as pleasant, such as the movements of the baby. Others may seem very unpleasant, like nausea. Familiar discomforts (like constipation or allergies) may become acute, or may disappear entirely for the duration.

This period appears to be one of physical discovery and adaptation. On the whole, most women feel themselves to be somewhat changed biological creatures from what they were before pregnancy. Those who are emotionally secure seem able to make this adjustment with less nervous irritability and strain.

Sexually anxious women are likely to experience more nausea, more persistent food cravings, more depressive moods and obsessive fears. On the other hand, women with happy attitudes about sex are more likely to experience a freedom from nausea, compulsive food craving, depressive moods and obsessive fears. In addition, they will tend to enjoy moods of elation associated with the pregnancy.

There is very little, if any, change in basic sexual adjustment during pregnancy, but there may be a slight decrease of sexual desire. Some women feel quite sad and guilty about this, and some husbands quite annoyed. It is a help if they are both prepared for a lessened desire of the wife, accepting it as a temporary state of affairs and one which the wife can do much to ameliorate by noncoital love-making with her husband.

Research shows that most women with previously satisfactory sexual experiences will want to continue some form of sexual expression throughout the pregnancy, whether or not their doctor has forbidden sexual intercourse in the last months. On the other hand, it also shows that women with sexual anxiety may use the knowledge of medical prohibition to cease all forms of sexual expression, whether or not their own doctor has applied this prohibition to them.

Interestingly enough, the sexually positive woman is likely to want her husband with her during labor, and later on to want to breast-feed their child. Contrariwise, the sexually negative woman is not likely to want her husband around during labor and tends to find breast-feeding unpleasurable, creating "acceptable" reasons for not doing it.

The consistency with which sexual anxiety is associated with various negative aspects of pregnancy and childbirth points up the need for therapeutic attention directed toward the elimination of such anxiety *before* launching a pregnancy. If ever a girl could profit from the help of a good marriage counselor or psychotherapist, this would be the time.

Of course, most normal women are aware of some specific fears and increased anxiety during a first pregnancy. The usual things they fear are the following: "Something may happen" to the baby (for example, malformation, monster births, stillbirth, or miscarriage); or they fear delivery (for example, anaesthesia, "bursting," or operative interference); or they simply fear "the unknown." Today, normal, healthy women rarely fear death in childbirth. Persistent anxiety is likely to be related to sexual anxiety. Obsessive fear is more likely to be related to guilt feelings carried over from some childhood experience, like having wished for the death of a little brother who may have died subsequently. It may be related to a recent guilt, like having entered the pregnancy unwillingly, or like having attempted an abortion. If a woman is suffering from obsessive fears, it helps enormously if she can talk about them to someone, preferably to a psychotherapist.

Education about the specific ways a woman may help herself during labor and about the specific steps the doctor is prepared to take to control pain, will generally relieve her *fear of pain*. Reading a book like Grantly Dick Read's *Childbirth Without Fear** or any of the more recent books written by advocates of Natural Childbirth is a great boost to the spirit.

In the appendix to my book, I have also listed several references which are enlightening and helpful.

Most pregnant women are told some old wives' tales by other women, seldom by men. These tales tend to feed the dominant fear of most women, namely, fear for the safety of the child. They represent taboos, or ritual acts to be performed so that "nothing will happen to the baby." Fortunately, most educated girls do not believe the circulated supersititions, though there are still people who tend to foist threatening tales upon pregnant women.

---

*Grantly Dick Read, *Childbirth Without Fear,* published in 1953 by Harper and Brothers, New York, N.Y.

Lack of intellectual interests during pregnancy is often complained of by intelligent girls. I have a letter at hand from one who wrote me thus:

"As pregnancy progressed, I became increasingly feeble-minded. Toward the end a vegetable quality pervaded my thinking apparatus, until the most intellectual literature I could manage were The New Yorker and The Reader's Digest. The New York Times every morning was just too much and I never knew then what was happening in the world of politics. The world closed in in indirect proportion to my belly's going out. At first I was concerned and thought that becoming a mother robbed one of all mental stamina, but later I didn't even care—not even when an old professor told me to have my head examined when he found me doing needle-point embroidery on a bathmat, after teaching me comparative anatomy and physiology."

As this mother indicates in her letter, slowed-up "mentality" is usually evidenced by lessened or lowered reading interests and disinclination for "intellectual" discussions. This is the time, par excellence, for detective novels. My husband solved my problem during pregnancy by coming home with his arms laden with mysteries.

An understanding partner can do much to reassure his wife that the slowing up of eager-beaver intellectual effort is simply par for the course. He might also point out to her the validity of the manner in which her intelligence is currently manifesting itself. It would seem as if it had gone to work on the internal and personal job of creation, and, in doing so, had caused the woman to lose interest in the external social problems with which she had previously concerned herself.

Emotional support from the father of the coming child seems to be the most important single factor associated with a serene and happy pregnancy for a woman. The influence of his sense-of-oneness in their joint enterprise finds its way into nearly every aspect of her feelings about, and behavior in, this new experience. Here are some comments by women I know as they told me of attitudes on the part of their husbands which had bolstered their morale:

"My husband took me to a movie and while we were watching it he put his hands on my tummy and laughed and laughed with pleasure at the baby's kicking. He's very sympathetic with me. Of course he teases me—says I'm his little apple dumpling, but he's so anxious for me to have the baby."

"He likes the way I look. I was tickled once when he said 'Darling, you look just the same from behind as you've always looked.' He is so tender with me, and has been all through."

"My husband speaks proudly to every friend we have about my pregnancy, and he always mentions to me how beautiful I look to him. He was delighted with the baby's activity in utero, and this pleases me beyond measure."

"I think my chief satisfaction in pregnancy is my husband's delight in it. He has been so anxious that the pregnancy be carried through to success. His appreciation of beauty in pregnancy has been a source of great pleasure to me. Through his eyes I've even come to think of myself as beautiful. I don't care how big I am. I think I'm wonderful because he thinks so."

"My husband wanted a baby even more than I did. He doesn't mind having me big. It isn't a beautiful thing, really, but it is to him. He wants to be aware of every change. He makes fun of me sometimes, like when I first put on a flannel nightgown. I looked pretty funny and we both shrieked with laughter. He's very conscious of another little person, too. He has never, in any way, been repelled by my pregnancy."

These comments offer a clue to the kind of need most women feel during pregnancy—a need which a loving mate

Pregnancy: Planned and Unplanned

can supply so simply and with such deep rewards to their marriage.

Indeed, the tenderness and approval that a man gives a woman during these months is remembered by her for the rest of her life. Many a woman, sustained by the love generated in her by her husband's attitude at this time, has been able to forgive and forget a thousand foibles committed by him at future times. Contrariwise, I have known many women whose love of their husbands was lost permanently by the lack of tenderness and appreciation during pregnancy. Some marriage counselors have called pregnancy "the first big hurdle" in marriage. I think I would agree with them. Certainly, it is a challenge to the emotional maturity of marital partners.

The coming of a baby elicits longings tucked away and nigh forgotten by both partners. When you first look upon your child, you want to take the earth by its tail and swing it. You want a perfect world for your treasure to inherit. You are filled with such a crazy pride that really isn't crazy at all. Also, you are so desperately tired. Thank God, being young, you have the energy to cope with problems.

There is a tendency on the part of both of you to focus on the Miracle and to neglect each other. This is a mistake, but if you are wise, you will soon learn. You will need to get used to a love of three, instead of a love of two; for what a baby needs more than anything else is to feel in the center of a radiating love between mother and father. My own children came to call this "being the meat in the sandwich," and they reached for it whenever they were tired or hurt. The mother and father need it, too, particularly the mother. The very nourishment of love given her by her husband provides *her* with the energy and impetus to nourish their child.

Almost no one tells young couples of the glowing joy of breast-feeding for the woman, both sexually and emotionally. Preorgastic excitation while nursing, however, is a familiar pleasure to experienced women, a rare few finding it so complete as to result in full orgastic release. What is not at all rare is the satisfaction and conscious enjoyment of diffuse sexual pleasure. This is enhanced by the loving appreciation of a husband.

I well remember one young man who confided to me a few weeks before the delivery of his child that the very thought of the baby nursing from his wife's breasts made him jealous, yet he knew that breast milk was the baby's "rightful due." Because he had the courage to try to understand his own feelings, and because his wise young wife could assure him that there would be room for *two* heads snuggled on her bosom, he completely changed his point of view. When the baby finally came, his greatest pleasure derived from observing madonna and child. He lost any sense of jealousy he feared he might have and seemingly, overnight, turned from boy to man.

Where there is a successfully nursing mother, there is usually an approving and supportive man. Perhaps one might generalize by saying that behind a successful man there tends to be a devoted wife and, behind a successful mother, there is likely to be a devoted and supportive husband.

13
Money: Coin or Curse

We think of money as the just reward for work accomplished. Actually, it is a tool invented by mankind for convenience, but not for enslavement. It can be the coin of happiness for you who are partners in love to the extent that you are in agreement about its control and management and have learned how to make it purchase that which you both find to be rewarding. You can be free of its possibilities for harm when you have resolved your emotional attitudes about it, dissipating those that are irrational.

When a young couple comes to me for counsel about money problems, I approach the subject in a way that would seem unorthodox, indeed, to an economist. For I assume that money can be equated to people's deepest feelings about a number of things, including power, authority, love, acceptance, rejection, superiority, inferiority, etc. Proceeding under this assumption, I suggest that our first task may be to discover what are the meanings money has to each member of the marital team. Just for fun, you might try this experiment for yourself.

Write down the word "money." Then jot down all the

associations you can think of that spring up in your mind in connection with this word. Take your time about it and be as honest and uninhibited as you are able. You may be in for some surprises.

You will find, I am sure, that power and control will be among your associations. Perhaps you will recover some feelings that you had as a child when you asked your father, or your mother, for money for some important purpose of your own and he or she questioned you too carefully about its use, forcing you to change your original plan in some significant way. Or perhaps you will remember when you had to pay for money with affection that you didn't feel for your father at the time, or with favors done for your mother that you didn't want to give. Perhaps you will find a memory of money taken from you as punishment for some misdeed that was utterly unrelated to your ownership of that money.

Perhaps money was a kind of god to the adults in your family, worshiped as an end in itself rather than as a means to serve them. Perhaps the reverse. It may have been spent so thoughtlessly that no one could feel that there would be any available for the big experiences or for emergencies.

Or perhaps one parent held the privileged position of spending all the family resources, using that position like a club, destroying any real sense of partnership between your parents.

Or money may have been in the class of unspeakable. Many Christian children have been brought up to regard money as "filthy lucre" or "the root of all evil"; a necessary tool of existence on earth but an unmentionable subject which "nice" people never talk about.

You may find that money is equated with being loved, with approval, with being rewarded by authority. Or it may represent rebellion against authoritarianism. "I will earn my own money and henceforth be independent of the odious control of those whom I do not choose to control me."

The list goes on and on.

Obviously, until you are quite conscious of what emotional roles money plays in your own life, you may make all manner of false conclusions about the use of it in your marital partnership. For example, when a wife, making her full contribution of labor and brains to her marriage, desires a joint bank account as a reflection of a real partnership, her husband may feel that he is "threatened" and "controlled" *if* he hasn't cleared up in his own mind the difference between his wife's present relationship with him and his mother's domineering one when he was a child.

"Would my wife really behave in the punitive way my mother did?" he has to ask himself. Of course, the answer is "No." But he will act *as if* the answer were "Yes," unless he takes the time to clarify the source of his feelings and to bring his present action into line with present reality.

Money does equal power. But it is power for a couple to use for the solution of their economic problems, not power for one member of a productive team to use over the other as a club. If it becomes the latter, the love relationship is damaged irreparably. Gradually, and insidiously, man and wife become enemies, each mastering the destructive craft of trickery. Anyone can see where this will lead.

The essence of a partnership based on love is trust, complete trust. Trust comes about not when we expect perfection from another but when we have a pretty good idea of the other's intent, his or her moral stature, and his or her past performance and when we know the kinds of emotional problems to which he or she has been exposed which predispose him or her to act in the ways he or she does.

Clearly, if John *feels* (without objective evidence) that his wife will take advantage of him if she knows what his total income is, that she will use her knowledge to limit his freedom, or that she will spend their income in ways that are not *his* ways he is not operating within a framework of trust, nor of love. If Mary *feels* (without objective evidence) that her husband's wishes always take precedence over her own, that she may be placed in the position of the little girl who had to "please papa" by begging for his favors or by paying for them in affectionate embraces, that he won't establish sufficient credit to keep her socio-economic relations with the butcher running smoothly, or that when he buys a bottle of liquor he is going to end up an alcoholic, she is hardly operating within a plan of economic partnership based on trust.

Both Mary and John have to realize that their money partnership is rooted in their love partnership. In an atmosphere of trust, each must become aware of the foibles, the attitudes, and the fears of the other, together taking steps to dissipate those that are irrational.

John, for example, may need to see that his fears about Mary are totally unrelated to Mary but stem from the days when he cringed over "loss of manhood" in his father as the latter succumbed to a selfish, domineering, and parasitical mother. Mary may have to see that her terror when John buys a bottle of Scotch has nothing to do with John's stability but, rather, arises out of her childhood fear of the consequences of her own father's alcoholism, along with exposure to her mother's premonitions of doom.

When Mary and John can expose their fears to each other, and when these fears are seen for what they are, then the relics of the past do not have to be projected into the future and Mary and John are ready to consider a positive plan for the management of family income.

At this point in a consultation, I usually say to the Johns and Marys something like the following, "It doesn't matter who manages the money in your team as long as each of you

Money: Coin or Curse 151

is represented on the Board of Control and has a voice that is heard and respected by the other."

Let the management fall to the lot of the one who enjoys it and has (or can develop) some competence in bookeeping, along with an orderly organization of records. Perhaps there will be an overlapping of interests and abilities. One may be especially competent in knowledge of investment practice. The other, in keeping the check stubs and paying the bills. The important thing is to decide on *who* does *what*, so that each can count with certainty on the jobs being done.

Next, how can the actual budget represent a true measure of fulfillment for each of them within their means?

In confronting a problem like this, I ask each member of a team to jot down a list of purchasable objects and experiences that each values most in life, in descending order. Never mind whether they represent necessities or not. Later on, we will deal with necessities. First, I help them clear up between themselves the order of emotional importance of expenditures.

Mary's list may look like this:

1. The cost of having children
2. A home that has some beauty in it
3. Attractive furniture
4. Good clothes
5. Travel
6. Good food

John's list may look like this:

1. Good food, steak at least once a week
2. A car
3. The cost of having children
4. A workshop
5. A nice, fat savings account in the bank
6. A home that we own ourselves

Our next job is to put the two lists together so that John can see Mary's ambitions and Mary can see John's. This is important, for if one partner is working the skin off his bones for a car and the other, working equally hard, has her sights on new furniture, neither realizing the objective of the other, there can be nothing but frustration.

Art and Ruth were an example of this. Art brought home a new car one night, without consulting Ruth, and expected her to be surprised and pleased. She was surprised, but not one bit pleased. In the misery of her self-pity, she nearly sank their economic ship by rushing forth to purchase (on credit) a new set of living room furniture. Their marriage was split wide open. It could have been headed for disaster had they not regained their sense of proportion in time to use this catastrophe to find a better way to attain their dreams.

Such a situation couldn't have occurred had they tried my little experiment of budgeting emotional values first and pooling the results.

When the joint list is completed, there still remains the need to itemize necessities: food, shelter, medical care, etc., for which there is a wide range of possible spending. With clear statements of emotional preferences staring one in the face, a couple can plan for the necessities with greater wisdom and satisfaction.

Food, for example, can be lavish or modest and still be nourishing. There is an even wider cost range on such items as clothes and shelter. If food is high on John's list and low on Mary's, they must arrange some kind of compromise. If Mary wants a satisfied John, she will have to include his once-a-week steak, if possible, and certainly she will have to give special attention to planning meals that he enjoys, whatever the amount of money spent. John will have to see to it that their lodging, however simple, reflects Mary's concept of beauty.

Clothing, for the time being, may be a carefully budgeted item. Travel may wait for one of those golden days in the future when their earning capacity is greater. What about the two important matters that were near the top in John's and Mary's lists: having children (Mary), and owning a car (John)? Can either of these be neglected? Indeed not. They will both have to be in the forefront of immediate objectives for saving. Both items will have to represent conscious goals that the two will work for together. They may decide which they will fulfill first, but this surely will have to be a joint decision.

Budgets arrived at in this way usually stick. They stick because in any contest between emotion and reason, emotion usually wins; in this case, the budget is built on emotional values, translated into terms that the intellect can deal with reasonably. Therefore, the budget itself is not resented as an unwanted taskmaster but as an implement for obtaining one's deepest wishes.

There is one word of caution I wish to submit to you most earnestly. Every living being needs some money for his or her own that does not have to be accounted for to anyone. In each of us there is a desire for independence which is frustrated when there is no leeway to act upon it. No matter how small your budget, allow to each partner a sum that is his or her own "independence" money. Let it be spent without conscience, wisely or foolishly, but, by all means, without having to render an accounting to the other.

What about the amount of money needed by any two young people to safely launch a marriage?

Many times engaged couples come to me with this question; some, even, who are earning a joint income of fifteen to twenty thousand dollars annually. They are afraid that this won't be enough to support them in marriage. This is ridiculous, of course! The attitude springs from the nonsensical hypnotic suggestion currently being broadcast in the world that one "must have" certain things in order to be happy. When young couples total up the price of the "musts," they are staggered, if not horror stricken. Some, lacking in courage, or believing all they hear, delay their marriage. Or worse, they may plunge into a binge of credt buying that mortgages their lives and their freedom for a long period of years ahead. When this occurs, they feel like slaves of the monthly payments instead of like independent souls, charting their own lives.

The plain truth is that unless your acquisitions reflect your real needs and your real purposes as you grow together, as well as your real capacity to pay for these, they are liabilities, not assets, for they impose too great a burden with too little satisfaction. On the other hand, if your possessions are within your earning capacity, and if they reflect what *you* want, rather than the stereotypes foisted on you by the pedlars of wares, they will represent the fulfillment of your purposes without precipitating unnecessary tension. They will, therefore, be enjoyable.

When you start out, all you really need is an ability to be self-supporting. If each of you has had a year, let us say, of such disciplined independence, you are likely to be good economic risks for marriage. In any partnership worthy of the name, both members are contributors to its economic and psychologic well-being. Both are producers. Until there are children, however, it is difficult for an unemployed wife to carry her full share of responsibility. One answer is a job.

Other demonstrations of responsibility also count as proof of ability to be self-maintaining, such as apprenticeships, disciplined educational achievements, management of a home, etc.

Jean came to me very worried because her fiancé was entering their coming marriage with a large debt incurred for his medical education. I assured Jean that she need not worry about this kind of a handicap. Jim had borrowed for a productive purpose and, with belief in himself, he had demonstrated his ability to make a plan and to accomplish his objective. His medical education was an asset that could repay the debt many times over through the years.

Sally, however, had a more legitimate reason for worry. Richard came from a wealthy family that had settled a sizeable annual income on him, for which he did not work and with which he did nothing productive. Yet he was constantly in debt. At the time of Sally's impending marriage, he owed ten thousand dollars, mostly representing "playboy" expenditures for elegance in furnishings and clothes.

I urged Sally to persuade her fiancé to agree to marriage counseling before entering their marriage. Much as she loved him, she saw that her marriage could only cripple him further if he did not iron out his irrational spending needs before handicapping a permanent relationship with such neurotic behavior. Because of his genuine love for Sally, Richard worked on his problem with a psychotherapist. He found that his need to indulge himself was rooted in his deep need for personal love and self-respect. His mother had entrusted his care to governesses and his father had paid him little attention until he entered preparatory school. There, so long as Richard conformed to plans set up for him by his father, all went well, but whenever Richard sought his own objectives, his father negated them. Richard's self-esteem was seriously damaged. Soon he found that he could get attention from his father by credit-buying, charged to father. Then, at least, he got negative attention. Presently, something worse happened. His mother invariably bailed him out of trouble as a way of vindictively getting back at her husband for his neglect of her. So a vicious circle was set up and Richard was the victim.

During the process of psychotherapy, Richard saw that he had been using expensive indulgences to himself as a means of bolstering his flagging self-respect and that he had never developed any real sense of being able to accomplish something on his own.

Sally, fortunately, was a very sensible girl. She patiently waited until Richard learned that he could be master of his own fate. Had she capitulated to his spending neurosis, she, and their marriage, would have been in for trouble. As it was, she was able to give Richard the love, approval, and encouragement that he really needed to help with his growing up. He got busy, found a job, took charge of himself, and developed an earned self-respect. Their marriage is now solidly on its feet.

Sally and Richard's case indicates that there can be neuroses involving money which are of such seriousness that psychotherapy is the only answer.

There are many calculated risks that all of us have to take in the accomplishment of any important venture in life, including marriage. But the accident that can break the backs of young couples is ill-health, physical and mental. You can insure yourselves against the economic handicap of the former by the expedient of relatively low-cost, comprehensive medical and income protection insurance. This is a *must* for any young couple entering marriage.

The only insurance you have, however, against the damaging effects of neurosis is the choice of a partner with responsibility enough, and love enough, to tackle the irrational aspects of his or her own character, preferably before your marriage. In our culture, marriage is a challenge for adults. It is voluntarily entered and it is based on the love of two people, each for the other without external compulsion. One criterion of the maturity of such persons to meet this challenge is expressed in the definition: "A person has become mature when he or she has become his or her own mother and his or her own father and stands ready to yield himself or herself up to the full hazards of independence."

Money: Coin or Curse

One hazard of independence is economic responsibility. It is also one of its privileges.

If you would establish a true partnership in money, as in love, these are the steps that I suggest you take:

1. Talk over your feelings about money with your partner.
2. Share knowledge of those of your aspirations that require the use of money.
3. Plan a budget tailored to your needs, emotional as well as physical, and not one based on a stereotype.
4. Allow for some independent spending within the framework of your income.
5. Arrange all savings and checking accounts and investments in your joint names, with a mutual agreement that any large expenditures not planned for in the budget will require mutual consent.
6. Decide on who will keep accounts and who will be responsible for investment, letting both be represented on the Board of Control.
7. When you run into neurotic problems relating to money, seek psychotherapeutic help.
8. Carry medical and income protection insurance unless you have some other satisfactory answer to the potentially heavy costs of ill health.
9. Do not mortgage your major goals in life to a standard of living that you cannot change should your values change.

14
Facing Up to Family Influence

Whether you are aware of it or not, you are marrying a family and a family tradition, as well as a person. You may be separated from that family by geographical miles; the individuals may be dead and buried; yet if you are honest with yourselves, you must ask, "To what extent are mother, father, grandparents still taking over in our own speech, opinions, actions, prejudices, and emotional flare-ups?"

For example, take the simple matter of eating. It is easy to assume that because you were conditioned to steak with onions, or beans with pork, or fish on Friday, that these combinations must be "right," as if ordained by an act of God. More men than are willing to admit it suspect that there is something wrong with their wives if they offer food which varies from that produced by mother. The palate of such a man, having been trained long before the development of his critical faculty, may retain allegiance to mother's cookery long after conscious attachment to mother's apron strings has been discarded. Else why does he insist on buttered toast floating in a sea of hot milk before bedtime, or crave tea brewed according to a special ritual?

Take another example. Why does a man feel himself less a man when he doesn't carve the meat at table, or ladle out the servings? I know a family where the children prefer to help themselves to the amount of food that each prefers, yet the kindly and otherwise emancipated father will again and again serve his wife and his youngsters as his own father served him. There is no rhyme nor reason to this. He just does it.

All of us are like this to a certain extent. We think we are free and independent beings, able to react to the exigencies of the present; yet we daily repeat compulsively those acts that we have absorbed, unconsciously, from our parents. If these are pleasing to our mates, or form a part of their own family patterns, well and good. If they violate our mate's notions of what is fitting and proper, the conflicts set up by our infantile dependence on the past must be resolved. Even when the backgrounds of two persons are culturally similar, there is often a wide sea of difference which can become a divisive gulf when one or the other insists on his or her own righteousness. Partners in love must build a bridge across these differences.

Make a study of your own prejudices and mannerisms brought from your past. This, of course, always begins with a negative and critical reaction on your part to some other fellow's foibles. Your own, naturally, are regarded by you as standard operating procedure; the other fellow has the idiosyncrasy. "All the world is queer, save thee and me, and sometimes even thee."

The next time that you are upset by a mannerism of speech, an idea, or the way someone does something, ask yourself, "Why am I upset?" Pursue the answer as ruthlessly as you can. See if your distress relates to a divergence of your way from his or hers, and then observe whether your way reflects that of your parents? Next, ask yourself, "How did this person acquire those mannerisms, those ideas, those ways? Was it from *his or her* parents?" Presently, you will step into a new and more colorful world. Not only are you likely to divest yourself of the rigidities of your own background, but you may come to have an appreciative awareness of people's behavior that will enliven your life rather than cramp it.

For example, there is a fisherman on the coast of Nova Scotia, where we spend our summers, who sends my children into stitches of laughter with his use of the phrase "a cam sea" (calm sea). If their regard for this man's general intelligence were shattered by the pronunciation of a word, they could invite a ruined relationship to a fine person, with great loss to themselves. What my children had to realize was that in this fisherman's world, the word "cam" was part of the folk language of the region and that their own English might seem queer to him.

"When in Rome, do as the Romans" may be simple enough a theory for successful operation outside the family, but between a man and wife it is not so easy. Each has friends, and a family, who are undoubtedly critical on some level. What we fear is the negative reactions of friends and family to the person to whom we are linked for life through marriage. This reflects our own fear of ostracism.

"What will my friends think," asked one girl who had come to consult with me, "when my fiancé says 'caint'?"

"Your fiancé has other qualities to recommend him, or you wouldn't have loved him. Trust your friends to find his likeable virtues. Would you permit them to inhibit your happiness by blindness that can't see beyond a 'caint'?"

She granted that she wouldn't. She also granted that her fiancé was flexible enough and intelligent enough to learn new ways of speech more appropriate to his present environment, provided she refrained from damning his background along with his "caint."

Every time we indulge in the cheap superiority of looking down our noses critically at the other fellow's foibles we deserve the trite verse with which my father admonished us as children:

> "There is so much good in the worst of us
> And so much bad in the best of us
> That it hardly behooves any of us
> To speak ill of the rest of us."

No one can know all there is to know at any age in life. No one has an option on the whole cloth of truth or taste, or culture with a capital "C." You and I may be aware of what fork to use at a dinner in the Waldorf, but I warrant most of us couldn't tell "a cam sea" from one that could "blow up to a lop" when a misleading sun still shone on azure waters. Our Nova Scotia fisherman can.

Does this diversity of skill make it impossible for deep communication, or for love to flourish? On the contrary, when we are confronted by a lack in our own knowledge, it is quite comfortable to say, "There is so much that I don't know. Please teach me." Or, when we confront another's ignorance, to say, "Would you like to know more about that?" Or, when we face diversity of social background, to bridge it with, "Would you like to know how this is done here?"

It is more difficult when ignorance is defended as *the* right, and this is apt to be the case between husband and wife where matters of family influence are at work. It is hard for us to acknowledge that our parents are not the paragons of wisdom and accuracy that we have imagined them to be. Because of this, we tend to defend the weaknesses of our parents, their ignorance, their unloved mannerisms, along with their loved ones! This is especially true when we have been critical of these things ourselves, for then it's as if we had been discovered in our own guilty secret.

Usually it is a good plan to refrain from negative comment about a mate's family, reserving complaint, if one has any, for one's own. The more one finds to appreciate in another person, including his or her family, the more he or she can expose his or her own weaknesses, including those of his or her family. On the other hand, if what your mate needs is the relief of a good "beef" about the folks, it pays to listen without coming to their defense.

Sometimes in-laws become real outlaws, and the going gets very rough. Your mother, for no apparent reason, becomes cross with his mother and lets you have the full blast of her criticism. For a while, neither parent will visit you while the other is a guest in your house. Or his father considers you a spendthrift and provides your partner with cogent "facts" to prove his point. Or your parents caustically comment that you are spending more time with his parents than with them and put pressure on you to take your vacation at the family homestead. And so on; the list is endless, but it all adds up to a need on your part to withstand negative criticism and to reject the pressure placed on you to do that which you don't want to do.

Subtle and not-so-subtle attempts at control are brought to bear on young couples by undisciplined and ungrownup grownups. I think that young couples have to resolve very early in marriage that they are on each other's team, first and foremost; that the well-being of their *own* new family is primary, albeit it seldom has to be achieved at the expense of anyone else. Nevertheless, where there are opposing interests, wife and husband come first.

The wife who places her mother's wishes above those of her husband's is too well caricatured to need much discussion, though it is appallingly often that immature girls fall into this trap. All that I can say to despairing husbands is, "Take your wife to the Gobi Desert or Tibet, anywhere beyond commuting range of her mother." However, a girl who hasn't tried to detach herself from the umbilical cord of her mother really isn't ready for marriage in the first place. The same can be said of a man.

How to wean yourselves from your respective parents and, at the same time, learn to know, appreciate, and love them *as people* is a task that you and your partner can tackle together profitably. It is well to remember that parents, on the whole, are extraordinarily "weathered" in the school of devotion. They are capable of generous acts of helpfulness and giving that you will seldom meet with elsewhere. Nevertheless, most parents have some trouble "letting go." Wherever they see you faltering, they tend to grab the reins. However, in the face of competence demonstrated on your part, they usually will stand aside and become a cheering squad.

The story of Matt and Margaret illustrates this. What *they* had to confront in weaning Margaret from her family may be rougher than what most of you will have to face, yet there are elements in their situation that I find repeated again and again in the young people who come to see me. In a sense, it is a classic story.

Late one night the phone rang as I was about to drop off to sleep. A minister, known for his sensitive approach to young people, asked if I would immediately talk with a young couple then in his study. "Send them along," I replied.

Hand in hand they came, obviously completely absorbed in each other and very much in love.

"Thanks for seeing us at this late hour," apologized Matt, "but we desperately need some help. I hope you don't mind too much." His engaging smile and tender manner with Margaret would have melted any last vestige of resistance to intrusion on sleep that I might have had. I stirred up the fire, brewed some tea, and we sat down to chat.

Margaret, with her hand still in Matt's, began to talk. The words came in a rush.

"I am twenty-two years old, and I'm an only child. I guess you'd call me 'the apple of my parent's eyes,' " she smiled wryly, "for all their hopes and dreams are centered in me, and it's quite a burden. They have taken precious care to see that I had the best of everything; only the trouble is that they are the ones who decide what that best is.

"I have been engaged for a year to Matt here. He is an architectural student. We have known each other for four years. I think he's wonderful, but my parents think he's not good enough for me. Dad says he'd like to shoot him, although he did give permission for the engagement. Mother converts every lovely thing we do into something tawdry, so that I can no longer enjoy it myself. This, in turn, infuriates Matt. But he tries not to get mad at mother because he knows how much I love her, and he doesn't want to hurt me. I feel so guilty if he utters even a word of protest about her. It's as if I had to protect my parents to 'pay' for all the wonderful things they did for me in childhood. This whole business leads to so much tension between Mat and me that we spend a great deal of our time just being anxious about pleasing Mom and Dad instead of planning our lives and enjoying each other. I get stomachaches every time I have to go home for a weekend or a vacation.

"Next year we both will enter a graduate school of architecture. We'd like to get married and work side by side in this adventure. At the moment, I am economically dependent on my parents, though I have had some experience in holding a job. Matt earned most of his way through college. Mom wants us to wait until we are through our architectural training before we get married. She insists that I live at home while I go to graduate school. Yet she dislikes

Matt so thoroughly that she gives him the freeze-out treatment when he visits me at home.

"During the past year our academic work suffered from the strain of being in separate colleges while we tried to solve our emotional problem with Mom and Dad. We don't see how we can stand the stress of three more years of this kind of underground warfare. On the other hand, we don't want to hurt my parents by our actions.

"Mommy says that she and Daddy have sacrificed for me and that I should remember how I might feel if either of them got sick or died while I was behaving selfishly. This makes me dreadfully afraid.

"Then she has a way of painting pictures of the outcome of any action we want to take, elaborating failure possibilities. The trouble is that her predictions are sometimes correct, so that now we begin to doubt our own good sense.

"My folks say that all they want is to be proud of me. I think I could make them proud if I weren't so tied in knots. As it is, I fail in nearly everything they want me to do. They think they've given me freedom to do whatever I please, but the real fact is that whenever my way leads away from their ambitions for me, or from them, our troubles begin.

"Matt wants me to marry him now. He feels that we could work for a year to earn our tuition for graduate school. After that we could work part-time while we study and thus finance ourselves through architectural training.

"I want to go with him. I feel that our lives belong together and that we have the basis for a good marriage. We are young and strong, and there is no area of our lives that we haven't enjoyed sharing, but then, there's that ghost of all those things that could happen to justify Mommy's predictions. And I get scared. How can I find my way out of this dilemma?"

When Margaret finished her story, Matt, who had listened quietly while she talked, now corroborated her facts, adding:

"Much as I love Margaret, much as I want her to come away with me now, I do not want her to act in any way contrary to her own convictions. I know that I could take care of her right now should we have to face an emergency, like a pregnancy. However, if we can postpone that for a while, I am sure that we can reach our professional goals and have a family also. We are both crazy about kids, you know.

"My folks are delighted with Margaret and completely approve of our marriage. Mother says that if she could have had a daughter of her own, she would have picked a girl just like her. They would help us financially, if we needed their help, but I don't want to depend on them in my marriage any more than I wanted to depend on them for my adult education. They have a right to their own hard-earned money.

"Are there good reasons why we shouldn't marry? Reasons that I've been blind to? Or can you help Margaret to see that in weaning herself from her parents she wouldn't be doing them any harm? Tell us frankly what you think?"

Margaret had described with graphic poignancy the dilemma of many sensitive, intelligent, but oversmothered young women facing marriage.

Here is the essence of what I told her and would want to say to any other young girl in similar circumstances were she to consult with me today:

"At the risk of shocking you, I have to say that unless you mature sufficiently to act upon your own best judgment instead of depending on that of your parents, you represent a liability to a marital partner and to a marriage. You place such a strain on love that you run a very real risk that the love itself may disintegrate for lack of the nourishment love needs.

Facing Up to Family Influence

Somewhere along the line, you have to be ready to say to yourself, "I have carefully surveyed the scene. I have weighed the consequences of desired action. I will take what comes. In fact, I will take responsibility for carving out my life circumstances and the very shape of what comes."

The things that seem to stand in the way of your doing this are guilt and fear relating to your mother and father.

It will help you to realize that the guilty feelings you experience when you contemplate action contrary to your mother's dream were carefully planted there by her long before the age of your conscious memory. She built them into you, so to speak, and you have a job ahead of you to wash yourself clean from their influence. They serve no useful function to you or your mother, and especially not to your fiancé. They are an unnecessary and hazardous burden.

Let's stand off a bit and take a more objective view of your mother and father. We'll assume that they do love you with all the affection of devoted parents, and that they did, indeed, bypass many a personal indulgence in favor of a large-sized investment in your future.

But they did this as an act of choice. What they did for you they did because they wanted that more than they wanted something else. They got more real pleasure from observing your flowering than from satisfying themselves with passing luxuries. Their "sacrifices" brought them satisfaction. If this was not the case, they were bargaining with life and you were the pawn.

Intrinsic in the rearing of any child is the understanding that parenthood is a process and a privilege, not a deed to possession. It is the act of nurturing a child of Life, not of persons. As parents, our deep and lasting joy comes as, little by little, we give our child up to life, observing him or her capable of increasing independence. If independence frightens us, we need to stop and ask ourselves if our parenthood is feeding some neurotic need of our own.

It is very clear that your parents, unconsciously, have used you to satisfy their own neurotic needs. To do them justice, we must assume that they mean well and that their false conclusions about their roles as parents derive from their own childhood experiences. Nevertheless, you must understand that it will not bring them either lasting happiness or health to stand by observing your life becoming as twisted as their own.

Of course, they tell themselves that what they want is your well-being. They repeat this to you emphatically, really believing it, but let us look at the results.

Observe yourself. You are an adult. You and your fiancé have had ample opportunity to test the quality of your love. You are both responsible, intelligent human beings with compatible goals in life and are strong enough to work out ways to reach them. Yet you have a stomach-ache every time you think of moving outside your mother's frame of reference. Whenever you make a choice derived from your own value system, it is denied by your mother's value system, and therefore spoiled for you.

Is this the result of liberating love on your mother's part? Or neurotic love?

Unquestionably, the latter.

Even her predictions of failure are operating like hypnotic suggestions. At present, it is she who is carving out your future, not yourself. If you choose to live in the house that she designs, you will always have a sneaking suspicion that it doesn't fit your dimensions, and, indeed, it will not. You must always expect to bump your head in the wrong places, for each mature woman must create her own emotional home.

Your salvation lies in the discovery of your own values which you will put to the test one by one, in the school of life. This is a process that will take time and physical separation from your mother while you are freeing yourself from her values and establishing your own.

Your economic dependence makes this more difficult, because the character structure of your parents is probably such that they may use money as a form of control.

If you risk your love for temporary economic security, you must, at least, realize what you are doing.

Your fiancé holds out to you a realizable alternative. He knows that it will represent work on both your parts and some hazards, with no one but the two of you to rely on if you fail. (Although, I might add, there is always help at hand for valiant spirits. Life seems to be on the side of courage.) Your betrothed, however, cannot put pressure on you to fly out of your soft but suffocating nest. Much though his heart moves him, he cannot urge you to go to some distant place where the two of you could try your wings without having them clipped at weekly intervals by your well-meaning keepers. For he knows that if you respond without inner conviction, it could end in recriminations. So he is, in a way, rendered helpless in the life-and-death struggle he sees you waging with your parents. He has neither power nor security on his side to lend weight to his convictions.

He can hear the rational argument of your parents, "Finish school first, and then get married."

However, he would be deaf if he didn't also hear the more rational argument, "If your parents will support you through graduate school as an unmarried student, why do they refuse to do so if you are married?" He knows that what they are really buying is three more years of your life for themselves; that this is what they want rather than your happiness or effectiveness in life.

Also, he sees the daily hurt they inflict on your hopes and dreams and he suspects that much more of this could utterly destroy your chance to fly with your own wings. And it could.

Your greatest expressed fear is of your parents' pain at your winging forth on your own and of their possible dramatization of pain through sickness or death.

Perhaps you should also realize that there is no greater sorrow for parents than to bear the burden of guilt that comes when they realize that they have strangled their child's chance or marital happiness through their own neurotic selfishness.

Should your parents, as you fear, have heart attacks, or other manifestations of distress, these may be looked upon as having been self-created and inevitable and may even be the nudge they need to take them to the proper professional resources for the real help they need with their real problems.

What now seems to them like a pain-giving act on your part may turn out to be the source of their ultimate joy.

If you will spread your wings in flight, you and your fiancé may trust the strength of your mutual love to carry you safely to a nest of your own making. Then, healthy life processes will probably heal your parents of any hurt your maturing may have caused them.

A month after my talk with Matt and Margaret, they were married. They asked for nothing from either set of parents, and they also took responsibility for their own wedding, inviting relatives and close friends to a simple ceremony performed by the minister who had given them the real help they needed at the time they needed it. They obtained jobs in a university town where they could continue their professional studies. Their housekeeping arrangements, while stringently simple, were adequate to their purposes and immensely satisfying to both of them. When last I heard from Margaret, her growing joy in their mutual deepening fulfillment is better reported in her own words:

"Our marriage is happier than I ever dreamed a marriage could be," she wrote, "but the thing that has really surprised me is Mother. She sought professional help for herself soon after our wedding, and what a difference this has made to all of us! Physically, she is healthier than she has ever been in her life, and she is paying attention to Dad, which is ever so good for him. They had their first real vacation together this summer since their own honeymoon. So it all turned out just the way you thought it might. I can't tell you how grateful Matt and I are. But I can tell you that we never lose an opportunity to send our hesitating friends to marriage counselors when they come to us with problems."

I have related this story at length because it includes so many of the emotional appeals that parents, out of their own neuroses, can make to a young couple. Some parents behave quite unethically. They represent the problem of *inlaws* turned *outlaws*. In this light, they need to be viewed. You never gain peace of mind or matrimonial happiness for yourselves *or* your parents by selling out to neurotic demands. You do better to ask yourself, "What, as far as we can determine, is a good solution for my partner and myself?" When you thoughtfully answer this question, you will generally discover that in the long run it is best for your parents also, however much they put up a dramatic protest at the time.

You must not get the idea, however, that I think that all, or even most, inlaws are likely to act like outlaws. The temptation for them to put pressures on young couples is very great in the face of indecision or weakness on the part of the young, but, on the whole, most parents behave with incredible restraint and forbearance, along with genuine love.

I would like to point out again that they can be a gold mine of rich information and advice. They can, and do, give services which cannot be bought at any price. They are a resouce for helping you to understand your mate in ways that you might never guess. Usually, all they ask in return is a little of your time and affection, along with an openness of heart on your part that is expressed in a willingness to listen. They don't even ask that you follow their advice, but only that you hear it, weighing its value as you might weigh the advice of a friend.

I know a great many parents-in-law who lament the lampooning that cartoonists give to inlaws. These wise elder citizens feel that this sets up prejudicial scare-aches in young sons and daughters-in-law which actually precipitate trouble when there needn't be any. I tend to agree with them about this. There is a funny side to all human frailty, but it doesn't help to create a hobgoblin in the minds of young couples entering marriage.

Many a girl and boy have told me of his or her gratitude to a parent-in-law who had come closer to behaving like the ideal of mother or father than had the blood parent. Also, I might add, it is often easier to respond without restraint to a love impulse with an affectionate inlaw than to someone in your own family. With the latter, so much emotional background, from which you may not be free, is involved that it may act as an inhibitive influence.

Often a husband can explain his wife's parents to her (and vice versa) so that she can really see them for the first time. These insights add to the maturity of the couple as well as to their love of their parents.

The subject of economic dependence on inlaws often raises its head. When, and under what circumstances, is it worth it?

In answering this question, I always ask a young couple one in return, "What is the price you have to pay for economic assistance? Are you willing to pay it?"

Facing Up to Family Influence

It is a mistake to think that there is no price to dependence, economic or otherwise.

If economic "grub-staking" is necessary, it is well for it to be set up either as an out-and-out business loan or as a gift with the "price" well defined and mutually understood in advance. Many young people and their parents feel that such underwriting is warranted when required as an investment in professional future—education, for example—or where matters of health for husband or wife or young children are at stake. However, most couples will tell you that it is rarely worth it solely for the enjoyment of a higher standard of living.

"Better a cottage achieved by your own efforts," they say, "than a mansion beyond your means for which you mortgage your right to independence of thought and action."

It is hard enough for most young people to gain the strength they need for independent action without jeopardizing that strength by attachment to their parents' purse-strings.

Money exchanges are wisely acknowledged in simple, straightforward, businesslike ways. This precludes the possibility of later recriminations such as, "I supported my son and his wife for the first ten years of their marriage, and now look what they do to me. I thought they would invite me to live with them in my old age, but the idea never occurs to them."

There is nothing wrong or evil about a written contract between parent and child. My hunch is that these are more indicated with relatives than with other people.

Should a young couple live with either set of parents?

Almost never is this wise at the beginning of a marriage. There is too much need on the part of the young husband and wife for the expression of feelings in ways that are not possible when other human beings are around, especially parents. Also, there is too much need to gain the self-confidence required to manage a home and to become parents in their own right. This confidence cannot be secured while a built-in bank of information lies handy and doesn't even require so much as a withdrawal slip to obtain. It's too easy to overdraw the account and then complain that their folks are dominating their life.

However, I have known of many a happy couple residing in close proximity to parents and parents-in-law—*after* the edges of a new marriage have been worn a bit smooth and the *second* child is on its way. The housing arrangement usually provides for the privacy of each generation. This generally means separate kitchen and bath facilities. Even then, contentment can be achieved only after a young couple has won its independence, rarely before; and only if both generations are able to approve and respect each other. The disciplined art of forbearance is rooted in a belief in the right of every individual to his or her own preferences, as long as these do not interfere with anyone else's right. If you can create such a fortunate relationship with your own parents or with those of your mate, you can risk living under the same roof with them. Otherwise, you would be wise to allow plenty of physical space between them and you.

How do you get your inlaws to understand your values?

You might start by letting them know that you *do have* values and that these are as meaningful to you as theirs are to them.

Many older people think that the young just don't have standards at all, that they act like will-o'-the-wisps, at the mercy of any wind that blows. So the oldsters, well-intentioned, jump in with their own recipes, which have worked for them (never mind how).

Facing Up to Family Influence

You can inform your families about your goals, and your general plan for reaching these. They may disagree with both, but they will see that you are people with a purpose, supported by information and experience of your own. In the end, you will have to claim your right to be wrong, which, in essence, is your right to grow. This is a claim that each one has to stake out for himself or herself, for no one gives it to another.

Values are changing rapidly in countless areas of life. Most of us tend to fix our parents' attitudes at some childhood level when we saw mother and father as rigid authoritarian dictators. We don't realize that parents are capable of changing along with the times. In fact, parents may be far more flexible than most young folks give them credit for being. It is worth a try to treat them as you might your most respected friends. Then, if you can't get your values across to them verbally, you will simply have to live these, hoping that in the end your family will appreciate your point of view. On the whole, however, the clearer you can be about why you believe what you do, why you want what you want, and why you do what you do, the greater their chance of ultimately understanding you.

With understanding, comes greater appreciation. With expressions of appreciation, comes deepening affection. Of course, it goes without saying that you must be prepared not to interfere with their lives either, any more than you want them to interfere with yours. "Live and let live" is the pearl of wisdom that will purchase untold riches for members in the larger family.

15
Work for Both Partners

No one feels adequate until he or she knows, beyond a shadow of a doubt, that he or she is a producer as well as consumer. This is not because of some abstract social theory but because it is the nature of humans to create that which one can objectively value and to value himself or herself in terms of what is created.

A person without work is like a bird without power for flight. Work gives life meaning, objective significance. Without it a part of a person dies. The greater the passion engendered by work, the more alive is the person, and the closer to the source of creation.

Not any work will do. Chores, for example, will not; nor will repetitive, brainless efforts of any kind, unless they are a part of a meaningful progression.

The finding of significant work, worthy of effort, is an achievement qualifying one as an adult. It is also a major qualification for a mature marriage. Curiously, some couples act as if it were not; as if it were, in some way, a threat to their marriage; as if a wife should be jealous of her husband's job, or vice versa. How inaccurate this is!

Work for Both Partners

The story of Rima and Hank will illustrate what I mean.

Rima came to see me, complaining that Hank had married not her, but his job. His home-comings in the evening had become later and later, his leave-takings in the morning earlier and earlier, till she said in jest that one night he would meet himself coming and going in the same hour. She lamented that she hardly knew her husband and that she, herself, had become so rebellious that she feared she might sabotage his work or abdicate from the marriage.

Hank turned out to be one of those heroes of industry who had built, by his own ingenuity, enthusiasm, and dedicated labor, a construction business with such a prodigious volume of production as to stagger the imagination. He loved his work; which is not to say that he did not love his wife and children. What he refused to acknowledge was that there could be any contradicition in terms. He had a valid point of view. No one could converse with Hank for thirty minutes and not absorb his contagious excitement for, and devotion to, his work *and* his family. To him, a worker and the fruits of his labor were the best gifts a man could give his loved ones.

Hank's absorption was no neurotic escape from boredom, nor was it a repetition of "What Makes Sammy Run." His was the legitimate fullness of passion of the man who knows what he wants to do and is busily involved doing it.

I helped Rima to take a second look at Hank. I urged her to ask herself what it meant to *her* to live with such a man. She began to see him as the unsung hero that he was, a giant of creative energy, converting it into productive use for himself and others. Then I asked her to imagine him sitting around the house of an evening playing bridge or watering the lawn. To her credit, she laughed. Later, she made other observations that took courage, yet her real love of him helped to open her eyes. She saw that he had absented himself from home more than he needed to because of *her* failure to accept his enthusiasm for his work, or to listen appreciatively to his reflections about unresolved work problems. She acknowledged to herself that she had greeted him with a "Don't bring your office home. Since you are so miserly with time, I want just *you* in the dribs and drabs of it that you save for me."

She saw that Hank had reacted in the only way a human dynamo can react, by removing himself further so that he could function without interference, coming home only for sleep, which was all of himself that his wife could accept at that time without criticism.

Then Rima made an even more important discovery; that Hank's work *was* Hank; in fact, had been the Hank she fell in love with in the first place. She found that she shared him most when she gave him the support of her approval. Not that Hank needed anyone's moral sanction, but a "well done" from his wife, or a glance that comprehended his struggle with any given assignment, were the life lines of emotional nourishment that could bring him to her doorstep as a bee to a flower.

Rima stopped complaining or asking for further attention as if these were her right. Instead, she learned to pack a lunch for two and to turn up on whatever construction job Hank could be found at, sharing his excitement over the production problems of the moment. She learned to welcome his tired body into her bed at whatever time of night he lay down beside her. She ceased to ask him to participate in a meaningless social life that drained his energy, but, from time to time, she joined him in celebrations that fitted his mood of "work finished." At these times, he brought her joy and gaiety unwithheld. Hank, in turn, gave her more and more of himself.

Rima found that the answer to unused time on her own hands was a job that could prove as engrossing to her as Hank's was to him. As their children were in school, she began to explore lines of interest that she had almost forgotten when the duties of a young mother had engulfed her energy. Now she was free to resume them, and presently she found her own answer to work. She invested herself in the discipline required to advance her skill, with Hank delightedly cheering her efforts.

Although Rima and Hank may have had fewer hours of each other's company, they have found a richness of association that is precious and sustaining. They have learned what all partners in love eventually have to learn, namely that two people can bring to each other only that which they are, and the greater part of what anyone is is what is achieved through work.

Some couples make such demands on life for security that they defraud themselves of the great joy of doing that which they feel to be worthwhile. This is the equivalent of selling themselves into slavery. Not that any task is demeaning if it is part of an orderly progression leading to a self-determined goal. But it is slavery of the most abject kind if it represents giving up satisfaction in work in favor of financial security. The latter is an illusive ghost that mocks happiness. But the couple that gambles its life on work meaningful to *both* has a reasonable chance to make it yield both security *and* happiness. At the very least, they have the wealth of having done that which they wanted to do.

I do not think that young couples today are as afraid of the big dreams, the long-term goals, as couples were in my generation. Partly this is because the partners in real love partnerships are not so saddled with rigid notions about who must do what.

In the past, social attitudes limited the ways each could contribute to the work partnership. A woman was expected to care for the home. A man was expected to earn the living. If there was a reversal of this pattern, the couple suffered censorship from its peers. Now, fortunately, both man and wife are free to contribute toward mutual goals in whatever way is required for success.

For example, a woman can work outside the home, helping to finance her partner through advanced technical training. Later, he can support her through childbearing. Later still, when their children have reached an age when they are outside the home more than in it, she can launch upon any further education she chooses, leading to her full participation in a business or profession during the later years of her life.

I know one superb woman executive who prefers her job to any form of domestic achievement. Her husband, on the other hand, loves to cook and is fascinated with the education of their children. They were miserable when they tried conventional roles, but when they reversed these, they found happiness. Both had to learn that what was good for each individually was also good for their work partnership. When they accepted this without guilt or apology to anyone, they were able to live in joy.

Two persons do need to be very honest with each other. Rock-bottom truthfulness of communication pays great dividends at this point. Partners in love have the opportunity of releasing each other to heights that only rewarding work can bring, but they are sabotaged at the start if they do not share their dreams.

Sometimes young couples face another problem. The man (or the woman) may have been through such castrating experiences in growing up that he (or she) really doesn't know *what* he or she likes to do. Under such circumstances, all work is a chore, because all effort through the maturation years has been dictated by what seemed like incontrovertible authorities. "Not my will, but thine be done" has been the theme song of their years, with the result that the individual has lost all sense of what his or her own will might be worth to him or her.

Work for Both Partners

What could the partner of such a person do to help him or her explore possible avenues of self-knowledge with the self-blossoming this brings?

She (or he) could treat the other's daydreams seriously. He or she could encourage the other to obtain the facts, skills, knowledge that might objectify an expressed hope and could refrain from saying, "That is crazy," or "That can't be done," or "You can't make money doing that." Above all, when an honest effort has failed, he or she could refrain from saying, "I told you so."

Sometimes it helps to ask, "Why did that fail?" or "What does your project need to help it succeed?"

Curiously, many persons fail to find a lifetime of rewarding work because they are defeated at the outset by a fear or distrust of *pleasure* being associated with *work*. This is part of the same "pleasure anxiety" that we saw inhibiting sexual fulfillment. The people who fear joy in work are those who were brought up on the theory that 90 per cent of life is made up of things that one *does not want to do* and, therefore, that must be done with good grace, as person's rightful duty. It is as if they said, in essence, "Work is work to the extent to which it is no fun." How can anyone find fulfillment within such a self-defeating principle?

Each person owes it to himself or herself to bring the keenest observation to bear on the discovery of what kind of work gives one pleasure to perform. To the extent that work, in itself, is pleasure-giving, to this extent can one devote oneself wholeheartedly to its successful outcome. Partners in love tend to work harder and produce more because love, itself, generates a positive energy, demanding transformation into creativity.

A woman needs satisfying and productive work, just as a man does. Throughout the ages, she has engaged in multiple occupations within the home that have made her an economic asset to the marital partnership. However, the tiny apartment in which the newlywed of today starts her marriage, combined wtih an industrial civilization that produces nearly everything more cheaply outside the home than in it, offer few challenges for youthful energy. Besides, it is very hard to stand by, marking time, till one can welcome a baby unless one can add one's own efforts to the realization of this goal.

However, it is distressingly true that even today a good many men set up a hue and cry about their wives working for someone else. Dozens of enterprising women still bring this problem to me in one form or another.

Some reasons these men don't want the women to work outside the home are as follows:

1. A man's ego may be involved. What will other men think of him? Particularly his father, his boss, or other men whom he wishes to impress (his wife's father, perhaps).

Some men have special difficulty in feeling "grown up," emancipated from the authority figures in their lives. To such a man, ability to support a wife may appear as a symbol of independence; whereas having a wife who is employed may seem to throw some doubt upon this ability.

If, as a young boy, he was only acceptable when he met his father's standards of behavior for him, and those standards now include the support of a wife, he may be plunged into emotional distress best described in the phrase "I'm no good," whenever he thinks of his wife on a job.

In a situation like this, she needs to make clear to him that a working wife is not a reflection of her husband's capacity to earn a living. Rather, it is a reflection of his *emancipation,* his *emotional security,* his *trust;* in other words, his *superiority.* She might point to the important men of our time whose wives do work, from presidents to corporation executives.

If she can do so gently, she might ask him how he felt as a child when he acted contrary to his father's ideas of "good" behavior. If he can tell her of the "I'm no good" feelings that engulfed him then, he may be on his way toward emancipation from childish dependence on other authority images.

Then, if she can speak positively of the kind of man who means "manhood" to her, a liberating person, generously appreciative of his wife's accomplishments (after all, didn't he fall in love with the girl who was, and is, working), she may be able to help him build some more adult concepts of the roles of men and women in today's world.

2. A man's possessive, competitive feelings may be aroused beyond his capacity to handle them. Perhaps he imagines that the men his wife will meet in business will surpass him in ability, or they will flirt with her.

Here the wife has another set of problems to deal with, though she may be sure that his flagging self-confidence is among them and that he feels threatened. There may also be a previous experience (probably in his childhood) in which trust in a woman was violated (or seemed to be). For example, I knew a little boy who lost three important women in his life through their marriage to other men, one after the other. The first was his nurse, the second his nursery school teacher, the third his kindergarten teacher. To each, in turn, he had given his full-hearted trust and love. As small boys do, he had entertained fantasies of marriage with them when he grew up. You can imagine how he might feel about trusting his wife in the company of other men.

It will never help to hurl an angry, "You're just jealous!" at a man suffering from jealousy. It will only reinforce his negative feelings about himself and make him cling more tenaciously to the illusion that keeping his wife safely at home will insure his own peace of mind.

What he needs most is to be impressed with her singleness of devotion to him, to be able to say to himself, "She chose me before *all* others—I have no doubt that she will continue to choose me." He needs to hear her celebrate his achievements, appreciate his successful handling of problems, feel her attentive interest in his professional development. If she comments on her boss at all, or on any of the other men she meets in business, she might take care to do so in terms that leave her husband in no doubt about her admiration for him.

Then, if she can speak often, and warmly, of his thoughtfulness of her, especially of her joy in his making her feel "like a woman," as contrasted with the workaday world in which she becomes just one more cog in the wheel of industry, he may quietly overcome his jealousy, particularly if she refrains from flirtatious behavior with other men.

It helps if she can remember that the task she is accomplishing is not simply the achievement of the temporary goal of keeping her job without his sabotaging it, but the more permanent one of building mutual trust beyond a shadow of a doubt. The so-called "female game" of keeping a man guessing may have value in cheap novels, but it adds nothing durable to a marriage. Freedom for both partners can be achieved only when the relationship is built upon the bedrock of deep confidence.

3. Religious influence and family tradition may have pointed stern fingers at a man, making him carry more guilt than he can bear if his wife works. Some churches, for example, recommend that a couple live on the man's salary because a working wife is thought to be a temptation to them both to delay "the responsibility of a marriage," namely, the begetting of children.

Here, a wife might point out to her husband that the reason for such an edict is to enable women to have and to care for children, which is her goal, also; and that the salary she earns through work will enable her to accomplish that goal more quickly. In such an instance, of course, she may have to agree to save her earnings for that purpose and not to use them for more luxurious living.

Family pressure is tougher to face, especially where the husband's father uses coercive measures when the prospective young couple does not follow his recommendations. In this case, it is *his* pride, *his* ego which is involved, *not* his son's.

How a man handles disagreements with his father is one of the important ways that he distinguishes himself from a boy. If he capitulates to his father, where his own better judgment dictates otherwise, thus permitting his parent to take over control of the marriage, a woman may want to give some further thought to entering such a marriage. Perhaps she would do well to wait until her fiancé grows up. Her very desire to postpone the marriage until he is emancipated from his father may be the needed leverage to help him to do so.

4. Some men may dread the fact that their wives may bring

home larger salaries than they do. In the early stages of marriage this is a real likelihood. A good secretary, for instance, may earn more than a young doctor.

If a young man is in this position, his wife could help him to understand the joy and the strength deriving from the "our" in their marital relationship and the weakness and uselessness of the "mine" and the "thine." She could let him know that she feels that whatever contribution each makes profits both, belongs to both, is earned by both.

She could remind him that there will be many times when she will earn no money at all, that she hopes, however, to make an equally valuable contribution to the well-being of the team.

She could assure her husband that the very meaning of marriage for *her* is involved in the concept of the "we" and the "our"; that it is never a case of "I earn such and such" but rather "We earn this income," whether the paycheck is made out in his name or hers.

I might add that it helps to keep as private between yourselves the distribution of the respective paychecks. If you must discuss your earnings with friends, let it be the joint income.

5. Some men fear that their wives won't want to be tied down to children if they get used to the freedom and independence of a job or the challenges of a profession.

In a case like this, perhaps a wife needs to express to her husband some of her deep, true feelings about the meaning of children to her. She might let him hear the longing in her voice when she tells him about her best friend's baby, or share with him her delight as she recounts a day spent with a child. Perhaps he needs to realize more fully the pleasure she anticipates in rearing his child.

If it is true that she doesn't want to be tied down to the routine chores associated with baby care, she might tell her husband of an alternative plan for the handling of those chores.

6. Some men are anxious about their own self-discipline and that of their wives in the matter of adjusting to one salary after having gotten used to two. Especially do they worry about their capacity to resist the lure of financial commitments that could not be maintained on one salary, though could easily be met with two.

Many young couples really do need two salaries to meet today's economic pressures. Often there are educational loans to be repaid, or capital required to launch a young man in business or a profession, and there is always some housekeeping equipment needed, though this is much less than most young people imagine. (If you doubt it, enjoy a good camping trip some time.)

The problem is to clarify goals, then to determine what is essential, rejecting the blandishments of advertisers and well-meaning friends alike. If a young couple succumbs to tempting burdens before taking steps to assure the ultimate attainment of major goals, both may find themselves with deep frustration.

Many couples decide, right from the start, to base their standard of living on the husband's earnings. This is the solution liked best by husbands who are concerned with the problem. These young people spend from the wife's salary only enough to pay for needed services in the home (to offset her labor there) and they save the balance.

A man is justifiably concerned about the financial responsibility which society still primarily hands to him in marriage. Also, in the back of his mind lurks the possibility of a pregnancy coming sooner than expected. No man likes to be caught unprepared.

7. Finally, many a man feels that his own need to be emotionally and physically cared for will not be met if his wife works outside the home. He may realize that the immediate years ahead will be full of stress and strain for him and that what he may need from her is a lot of tender, loving attention. I might add that she experiences the same need from him if she works.

It is true that in today's work world there are many pressures that take an extraordinary toll in terms of emotional exhaustion. This depletion needs to be restored somehow. Many a person entering marriage counts on the partner to be the means through which the restoration occurs, and this may indeed be one of the great contributions that each can make to the partnership.

Certainly, every person being buffeted about in the abrasive world of competitive business, needs some healing. And how can a man ask from his wife that which she needs as badly as he? If they both work, who will have the energy for the art and effort of emotional and physical renewal?

Work for Both Partners

One man said to me, "I want to fall into my wife's arms when I get home from work. I want her hands kneading the kinks out of the nape of the neck, and I want the smell of dinner on the stove and a cocktail in the cocktail shaker. I want to be somebody's spoiled and petted darling for a few hours each day. If I know that my wife has had the same stresses to meet in the world of work that I have, my conscience won't let me indulge myself. Yet the pressures on me are so intense that I need this kind of bolstering of my spirit and release of my body's tensions. It's one of the gifts of love that the Japanese girls knew so well how to administer. In the army, when we were stationed out there, we basked in it, and I, for one, made a private resolve to find a wife who could give it to me."

Somehow this need must be met, both for men and for women who invest so much of themselves in the business and professional world. It cannot be bypassed for long without paying the price of serious depletion.

There are, however, many ways to accomplish physical and spiritual healing. I teach young couples how to rub each other's backs, how to use massage as an aid in unkinking the nervous knots created by tension in a high-pressure world. I also try to dislodge any puritanical, self-depriving notions either may have about engaging maid service to replace the wife's labor in the home, or, for that matter, about other "indulgences" that heal frayed nerves and wounded spirits.

However, the smile of greeting, the "well done" with which each acknowledges the work of the other are among the greatest renewers of energy in this world.

16
Religion in Marriage

Spiritual adventure lies at every person's doorstep. When a man and his beloved cross this threshold together, a deeper level of living opens for the two of them.

Religion represents a person's attempt to understand the meaning of life. *Ethics* represent the effort to act in accord with that understanding.

I think it fair to say that most of us reach adulthood with a set of ready-made answers to both religion and ethics. These seldom represent our claim to personal conviction in any sense of the word except that of emotional compulsion. They are our inheritance from mother and father; gifts *given* to the immature, to children. They are *not earned*. Nor are they ours until we have opened our own inner doors to spiritual awareness and have committed ourselves to the life-long search for truths of the spirit.

Such commitment is one of humanity's greatest adventures. When joined by a partner in love, it is a well-spring of exaltation seldom found by the solitary seeker.

What a pity that so many marriages bog down at the level of compulsion about codified expressions of religious experience! So many people confuse religion with church, truth with the laws of the Scribes and the Pharisees, spiritual awareness with submission to prescribed ritual. Out of this confusion, many partners in love are blinded beyond capacity to join hands in a search that could illumine their lives.

Consider this problem through the eyes of two young people:

Ruth and Lee are engaged to be married. Ruth has been reared in the Jewish tradition; Lee in the Protestant. Ruth assumes that she is a Jew; Lee that he is an Anglican. But what does this mean? Do they have a religious difference, or is the difference one of cultural experience, reinforced by emotional equations learned in childhood and to which, out of fear or lethargy, they tenaciously cling?

If Ruth and Lee have delivered their spiritual lives into the hands of their ancestors at the very dawn of their own adulthood, they have little chance for a partnership in religious growth. On the other hand, if they realize that they have come to this threshold with an emotional inheritance that now must be tested for its power to transmit courage and joy, they may earn a spiritual partnership rewarding to both of them.

How should they begin?

First, they must recognize the difference between a ritual and a creative act which expresses their personal reverence for life and for love. The two can be synonymous, but often they are not. Just as words may mask meaning, so can dogma mask spiritual truth. There need be no contradiction, but if there is, the validity of the dogma must be questioned.

It is a great help if Ruth and Lee will subject themselves to a study of the great religions which form our cultural heritage. All schoolchildren should, at some point in their education, be exposed to the history of religious thought, just as they are exposed to the history of battles, politics, science, and art. Unfortunately, we treat religious ideas as if they were something divisive and sacrosanct, which is a mistake. All organized religions are administered by human beings. As such, they reflect the best and the worst of which people are capable.

Ruth and Lee might examine the forms into which religious experience has frozen; for example, religious systems and churches.

Our temptation to systematize and to organize, along with our presumptuous notion that we can "give" religion to our children instead of helping them to earn their own, has led us to concoct images and symbols which have been passed on from parent to child. Actually, these are substitutes for direct experience. Certain acts, like coins, are assumed to be exchangeable for spiritual grace. Can Ruth and Lee use any of these today to give their lives substance? Are some counterfeit and some pure gold for them?

If Ruth, for example, refrains from eating ham, does she gain some special strength from the active contemplation of an ancestor's courage and foresight at a time when pork was likely to be unsanitary and therefore tabooed? Or does her action merely reflect an emotional scare-ache masked as "religious observance"?

If Lee eats fish on Friday, does he do so in joyful celebration that the world once contained a man whose love was contagious enough to persuade a multitude to share their loaves and fishes? Or because he retains a fear of nonconformity?

Can Ruth and Lee permit to each other whatever ritualistic acts each finds useful in enhancing ideals? Or does one scorn such acts in the other, using that scorn as a divisive weapon? They grow in love when they mutually appreciate each other's needs. Their lives wither as from a dry wind when they become judgmental.

What are Ruth and Lee to do about pressures from their respective churches to act in ways contrary to their own convictions, or even, to their own best interests?

It may seem strange to speak of any church as a "pressure" institution in a country dedicated to religious freedom. However, we have to face the truth that occasionally in our United States churches have exerted coercive control of the private and personal lives of people who have not submitted voluntarily.

In my own New England village of Sheffield, there was a moment in history when anyone who did not belong to the village church was made to pay a fine.

Within the legal framework of our nation, can Ruth and Lee decide what is the Good and the Right and the Just for them, accepting the dictates of their churches only to the degree that the latter conform to the former? If so, they have little to fear from a difference of church membership.

Ideally, a church is a fellowship of people seeking to understand the nature of God and the universe and to live in accord with the spiritual laws that have been revealed to them. Their worship is an affirmation of their conviction. The congregation gives the members mutual support in that affirmation.

Most of us need all the emotional support we can get. If a church fellowship affirms the best we are capable of; if, in compassion, its members help to lift each other out of the morass of failure; if it is a human resource for the sharing of joy and sorrow and for the celebration of our most solemn deeds, it makes a contribution to humanity's life on earth that is incalculable.

If, in addition, its professional leaders are trained to offer the skill and can give the love required to teach human understanding, a church can provide emotional life insurance to a whole community.

I believe that the day will come when every church and

temple will have a pastor, priest, or rabbi schooled in the disciplined art and science of psychotherapy. Such persons will help to pass on the knowledge necessary for men and women to live together in love.

A church can also be a first-aid station for rendering assistance to individuals or families in distress. A minister, for example, is the first person I think of when I am looking for practical help for anyone in the neighborhood. He or she knows who has what jobs to offer and those who are in need of a job; who has a spare bedroom in her house and also a heart big enough to welcome a pregnant girl in need of temporary shelter; whom to enlist in community causes that require workers; who can cheer a person sick in his or her soul; who can get quick medical help for someone in need of it—and so on.

The church, unlike a social agency, is not tied to the rigid limitation of "agency policy" but can say, "Wherever your need lies, there will we, your neighbors, try to lend a hand. In return, we ask that you lend us a hand when we have needs." This is a fair approach that does not smack of charity. Self-respecting men and women can be a part of such reciprocal arrangements and under these terms they can say, "Ask and it shall be given you."

Because almost every family needs emotional or physical help at one time or another, it does have an obligation to be a part of giving it. One way to do this is through church membership.

If you and your mate decide to join a church, pick one where you like the people as well as its way of worship, but remember that church members are still human beings with human frailties and foibles. You, along with like-minded friends, will have to take your full share of responsibility for creating the Body Spiritual, which will be as effective or ineffective as you and your neighbors make it.

The professional leader of that church, be it minister,

Religion in Marriage

priest, or rabbi is neither a servant of his flock nor its conscience. He or she is a highly dedicated, professional person, trained to offer you knowledge of his or her particular religious system of thought and worship and to render guidance when you are searching for spiritual insight. The ministerial function is not to control you in an authoritarian way, not to be an arm of Jehovah, but a person who may possibly point out some signposts that may be fruitful in your own search and growth.

Do you and your mate talk over your own thoughts about the meaning of life? Or do you keep silence before that which you imagine are the imponderables?

"What do you think God is?" I sometimes ask young people who have come for premarital counseling. I ask it as a way of acknowledging that every living soul does ask such questions of himself or herself if only within the deepest reaches of consciousness. Too often one fears to expose these reflections to the beloved, yet partners in love deepen their love through such exposure.

Together, dare to open your minds to the imponderables. Believe in your own ability to discover spiritual laws. These determine how you live far more effectively than any laws of the land you live in. Church leaders have no option on spiritual truth. A few may even be mired in the ruts of ancient wagon tracks that lead nowhere. Take charge of your own life, following the green lights as you see them. These may lead you to insights that will illumine your life as well as strengthen your partnership in love.

A spiritual truth is a workable law of life that brings you closer to happiness, love, health, and to other sources of creativity. Some might say "closer to God."

Partners in love, searching for spiritual truth, find it in the most surprising of places.

One couple may discover it in unspoken prayer for their critically ill child. As they reach out in love toward each other, affirming the child, he stirs, his fever breaks, giving promise of a new hold on life. The touch of their expressed love is actually healing. Jesus spoke of this nearly two thousand years ago, but this man and this woman discover it at just this moment.

Perhaps a woman finds her first earth-shaking awareness of union with God as she loses herself in her husband's embrace. Sexual communion contains within it the potential for total abandonment to the Beloved. Suddenly, into this woman's consciousness is born the significance of the statement, "Whomsoever shall lose himself shall find himself." It is now her personal discovery.

Perhaps a spouse finds, as all wise spouses do, that he or she cannot be all things at all times to the mate. He or she needs something from another's hands. Instead of yielding to a jealous impulse to insulate him or her from the personal gifts of others, he or she makes these possible. A greater level of joy is experienced in a mate's fulfillment. The partner has not had something taken but he or she feels that something has been added. In new confidence, one learns that "whatever is right and good for one person is usually right and good for those with whom he or she is in personal relationship."

Perhaps a father discovers, contrary to popular precept, that if he sacrifices something to his son which is essential to himself, the son cannot receive the gift with joy. Suddenly he senses a new meaning in the shepherd's psalm "My cup runneth over." He begins to understand that acceptable gifts can come only out of filled cups that *can* run over and not from the dregs of empty ones.

On and on the list could go. There is a never-ending trail in this land of learning. As you walk it, hand in hand with your beloved, problems such as differences of church background, rites, and rituals will become of less and less importance before the larger issue of your lifelong search for ways to objectify God's universe upon this earth.

17
Wayside Shrines

> "While God waits for his temple to be built of love, men bring stones"
> FROM *Tagore*

"Their marriage is a Mutual Appreciation Society," commented Jean, as she described Laurel's romance with Bill.

"There could hardly be a better Society for a partnership in love," I responded.

"Well," she continued, "they're celebrating their twenty-fifth wedding anniversary tonight and the two of them need heavy things to hold them down. Laurel always was a handsome woman; now she is radiant. Everyone looks at her a second time. As for Bill, he just glows. The men say he is the most productive man in the business."

Through these mature lovers, Jean was identifying an emotional "vitamin" so essential for the nourishment of lasting affection that I doubt if any marriage could long endure without it. The ordinary person takes such a beating in the workaday world that any surplus of self-appreciation is soon depleted, and needs replenishing. A marital partner who can add to the good self-feeling of the mate is life-saving, as well as love-saving.

I know a man who frequently writes love letters to his bride of thirty years standing, though he lives in the same house with her. His notes, like joyous candles on a birthday cake, light up her eyes with a warmth that radiates back to him.

I know another man who keeps a loose-leaf notebook in a special drawer of his desk, to which only his wife has entry. Into it he copies the soul-inflaming, thought-provoking lines he discovers in the course of his own reading. Whenever her spirits droop, she finds winged words there that lift her eyes from the ruts in the road to the hills beyond the ruts.

There is no end to such pathways to mutual appreciation. The more varied and original these are, the more adventurous the marriage.

A man, surprised by a breathtaking sunrise, awakens his wife to share its beauty. He wants to bring her into the orbit of his expanding consciousness of splendor. He is really saying, "This burst of color is for you."

A wife, stepping outside her door when the northern lights are dancing in the heavens, calls to her husband to watch them with her. She is really saying, "Come, I give you this extravaganza of the gods."

Such gifts of appreciation, glorious as they are, demand confidence in the receiver to receive. A depreciated gift discourages further giving.

A young man said to me recently, "I don't think many women really like to cook; they only do it to please men."

Though he was not entirely right, there is an element of truth in what he had observed. Appreciation from another may well give cooking its zest for a chef.

There is no act we do, great or humble, that is not enlivened by a word, a glance, a gesture of appreciation. These are the singing melodies that add a lilt to our days and lift our feet in dance. Like a Scottish platoon that marches many a dreary mile when the piper plays a tune, so is a marriage winged with appreciation.

Women complain about lack of appreciation more than men, perhaps because much of their traditional work is repetitive and therefore less satisfying. It is also less subject to praise. Furthermore, men, being more inhibited by the tenderness taboo, often find themselves tongue-tied and thus less able to give their wives praise.

On the other hand, I have known many a man who hungered for a compliment from his wife. And "hunger" is the proper word, for there is a sense of actual body emptiness when one suffers appreciation-deprivation. Some people who overeat do so because they lack approval, and certainly we know that almost no one can flourish in an atmosphere of criticism. The hypercritical mate is just about the poorest marital risk there is. If such a person marries at all, his or her marriage is likely to shipwreck on a shoal of ice congealed by the chilling effect of his or her own criticism.

On the other hand, we gravitate to those who show that they like us.

A fourteen-year-old girl asked me a question one day that is the commonest question asked in any teen-age group or, for that matter, in any unmarried group of adults. "How can I get a boy (or girl, or man, or woman) to like me?"

My suggestion offered her a clue which brought her spectacular results when she tried it.

"Find a boy," I said, "whom you would really care to know. Then think of a dozen things that you truly like about him. Be explicit and observant of that which he has achieved by his own efforts. Next, find some way to let *him* know that you have noticed and approved these positive things about him."

It's a rare boy (or man, or woman) who doesn't respond with warmth.

Appreciation, I might add, is very different from flattery.

Flattery is based on scheming and is always self-seeking. Appreciation, on the other hand, is based on truth and is self-sharing.

When the teen-ager's question is asked in any of the Marriage Preparation classes which I teach, I play a game with the group members that gives them a lively demonstration of the effectiveness of expressed appreciation. It goes like this:

"Will each of you please look at your neighbor on the left," I instruct. "In one minute, I am going to ask you to say to that neighbor something that you have found likeable about him or her. Next, I am going to ask *him or her* to respond in a way that makes *you* feel glad that you have brought your gift of appreciation."

At the outset, there are usually giggles, masking anxiety, but also a noticeable eagerness for the game to proceed. As it gets under way, a new level of good feeling permeates the group. Never has it failed to produce happier relationships among its participants. I recommend its daily practice to partners in love.

There is another kind of appreciation that is often neglected, yet its practice differentiates the mature partner in love from the neophyte, the woman from the girl, the man from the boy. It is the gentle acceptance of the foibles of the beloved, combined with an appreciative response to them. This is quite different from "tolerating" what may seem to some as a "weakness." On the contrary, it is a positive acknowledgment of human need that transcends concepts of weakness, letting these foibles be openly admitted without shame or guilt. They are catered to and acted upon with love, endearing the partners to each other.

Here is an example of what I mean:

Maggie was sorting socks in her husband's dresser drawer one day when she came upon a packet of French postcards (the usual collection of provocative female nudes). At first, she was quite taken aback. Presently, however, as she considered the significance of this revelation, her appreciation of her husband's uncommunicated need increased. This and her sense of humor guided her subsequent action. Sprinkling some of her own perfume on the photographic ladies, she returned them to their envelope, along with a note that read, "For best results, try Maggie."

With a light and loving touch, Maggie had been able to bring "out from wraps" her husband's shamefaced enjoyment of a hidden stimulant. She had said, in effect, "I like you however you are and you don't have to keep any part of yourself secret from me."

Appreciation pays an added dividend. Wherever it is given, it evokes further appreciative responses, affectional in quality. Just as food and oxygen are converted into fuel for the body, so is approval fuel for the spirit. As we consume it, we even breathe more fully and deeply, and this kind of breathing is, in truth, the breath of life. It adds to our well-being on the physical level as well as on the spiritual. It becomes a life-giving, love-giving element which partners can make abundantly available to each other.

As I have talked at length about the value of emotional and spiritual nourishment, I would like to say a word about physical nourishment through food itself.

Our grandmothers may have lacked knowledge of modern psychology, but they had one basic wisdom which served them well. They knew enough to feed a hungry man.

Food and oxygen are the primary fuels which stoke the furnace of that *energy system* known as a human. If one breathes shallowly or goes on short rations, one becomes a grumpy, negativistic pessimist. Most spouses realize this, but many fail to act upon it. Some of the grimmest tales brought to the marriage counselor are enacted on what are, essentially, empty stomachs.

A husband comes home and his wife isn't there. He

reaches for a cocktail to provide himself with a quick renewal of energy, then dives for a comfortable chair in a belligerent and disappointed state. In comes his wife to a growled greeting and she (also hungry) strikes back with, "You just want to keep me a prisoner in this house. You resent it when I have an afternoon out with the girls."

Quite wrong, of course, but an unpromising start for an evening of shared love, which is what they both really hungered for.

Contrast this with a home I visited recently. The husband was a colleague, and as we were working on a project that we didn't want to interrupt, he took me home to lunch with no advance warning to his wife. When we arrived his wife was not there, but on the table was as delightful a fare as one could wish, along with a note from her that read, "Dearest, enjoy your lunch. I'll be back as soon as I can. Have gone shopping with Margaret. Love, Mary." Mary's love was present in her absence, and Tom felt it.

Every husband-wife team needs a good cookbook. After the Bible, it is the first book that belongs in their library. I would also recommend Jean Hewitt's *Natural Foods Cookbook** for a delightfully informative account of the relationship of nutrition to the maintenance of general health.

Whoever chooses the responsibility of feeding a family must take the time and make the effort to understand the vast differences in qualities of food. This person must also arrange to have snacks available to every member of the family when needed. The little hand in the cookie jar (what kind of cookie?) and the larger one in the refrigerator (what will it find there?) are symbols of satisfied people. The source of that satisfaction is a loving person, and his or her act is felt as an act of love. Food deprivation is experienced as a gesture of hostility or punishment. It is well to remember this when you wonder why your partner is angry some night when he has arrived home to a woman-absent, food-empty house, however much he may pretend to shift the reason for his irritation to something more sophisticated.

I am a great believer in these nourishing snacks, readily available. They can be slipped into the hand of your yowling youngster, or given to your mate when he or she comes home with drooping shoulders, or enjoyed by yourself at a moment when the world's problems loom big. They make *all* the difference! Whoever invented the timely cup of tea deserved canonization among the household saints. I feel this so strongly that I never let anyone tackle a marital problem in my office it I know that he or she has come there on an empty stomach. I insist that *first* we eat and *then* we work on problems.

Along with the lure of food and appreciation, that of fragrance draws us as does a magnet.

For a number of years, I directed a nursery school located in a socially sophisticated neighborhood just off Fifth Avenue in New York City. We had a cook who made home-baked bread for the youngsters. On baking days a steady line of parents and passers-by followed their noses to the kitchen door, always asking, with nostalgic looks in their eyes, "Can visitors come in?" "Do you sell bread here?" "Can I have a taste of whatever it is that smells so good?" Once, when we threatened to remove the kitchen to an upper floor of the school, a famous psychiatrist cautioned against it, saying, "No don't. The smell of that bread coming out onto the sidewalk is enough to overcome the fear of any timid boy or girl as he or she breaks from the mother's apron strings and enters the awesome new world symbolized by the schoolroom door." So we left our kitchen downstairs, and with it, our neighborhood magnet.

Everyone cannot bake bread today, but there are thousands of fragrances with which we *can* fill our homes to satisfy our senses: a pine bough, a wood fire on the hearth, a cake baking, a stew brewing, lilacs in the spring, and so on. And there are personal fragrances drawing man to woman and woman to man. Experiment with these to discover those that appeal to your partner in love, for the sense of smell provides another open avenue to expression of affection that is too often neglected, as if it didn't exist.

Expecially beware of odors that offend. These drive the most warm-hearted lovers to opposite sides of the bed or to far corners of a room. Bodily uncleanliness, dirty underclothing, sweat-soaked shirts, bad breath are a few of the more common. These may seem too obvious to mention. Yet is is surprising how many men and women complain to the marriage counselor about such well-advertised "unmentionables." Because they represent elementary learnings, grown-up sophisticated adults tend to interpret their presence in a mate as a deliberate act of sabotage and resent them bitterly, and often silently.

If your mate has indulged in thoughtless slovenliness, it won't hurt a bit to let him (or her) know that he or she can give you a great deal of pleasure through your nose and that you don't like to do without this delight. I know one wife who takes her tired and smelly husband by the hand, as she might a weary child, and draws a hot bath for him, washing his back and laying out his clean dressing gown, as an act of love. He gets her message, but in a way that he can accept, for it contains not one hint of reproval or criticism.

Many of us are still rebelling against fastidious and interfering mothers who have put cleanliness ahead of godliness. Then we enter marriage, taking out on husband or wife the rebelliousness of our childhood. Loving humor and an expression of your real delight in the fragrance of a body so fresh that you can nuzzle under armpits or drink in breath, helps a mate discard such infantilisms.

One man told me that he had been "put-off" marriage for several years when he was in his early twenties, after living for a while in a house where there was a new baby. The wife didn't know how to attend to diapers so that they wouldn't permeate a house with the odor of urine. "If this is what one has to endure in marriage, it's not for me," he had said to himself. It wasn't until he discovered that such odors didn't *have* to be associated with babies that he could bring himself to embark upon marriage.

A man who brings his wife perfume is saying "I like this. I want to associate it with you." She would be wise to welcome this communication. On the other hand, there are many men and women who do not like perfumes. It is well to find out one's partner's preferences.

I often ask each member of a marital team to list all the fragrances that each can think of that make him or her feel good, that relax, that lure; then, to make another list of those that upset, that repel or make one move away, almost against the will. Next, of course, I ask each to share this list with the mate. Most couples are quite surprised. If they are willing to act upon this knowledge of one another, they find rich sources of new pleasure to give each other. Needless to say, such mutual awareness helps to eliminate a source of displeasure.

Along with the lure of fragrance is that of candlelight and color, for most of us are artists at heart, craving the beautiful. Although a man may want a good light to read by and also insist that he be able to *see* what he is eating, a candle on the table, along with eye-filling, soul-warming color in his home will call out to the quality of joyousness in his spirit. Most people think of happy experience as being "colorful" and sad experience as being "gray" or somber.

Home decoration is a learnable art that every man and woman can acquire. In its essence, it is a reflection of the inner person, yet the inner person is also shaped by external circumstance. Beauty in the home brings a sense of peace, of harmony, and of lightheartedness.

One of the delicate adjustments two people in love *have*

to make lies in resolving their respective tastes. Because we have differing emotional reactions to color, for example, this is one element that especially needs to be taken into consideration.

If Mary paints the bedroom wall pink and John turns bilious whenever he looks at pink, the problem this can raise is obvious; or, if John's differing tastes prevail in the selection of their furniture, you can imagine the lack of personal involvement Mary may feel about its upkeep.

As in the matter of fragrances, partners in love need to "talk out" their preferences in color and decorative style. What they end up with need not be a "compromise," for compromises are rarely satisfying to anyone. Instead, motivated to please each other as well as themselves, Mary and John may arrive at a brand new solution, fully delightful to both. Whatever effort this involves is worth the struggle. Perhaps the den will be John's, from start to finish; the kitchen, Mary's. Perhaps they can combine their tastes in a mutually pleasing whole. But whatever their solution, like everything else in a marriage, it needs to be one that both are happy about.

A constant source of irritation occurs when one mate spreads his or her possessions about and then, after being drafted away to another activity, returns to find that the work in progress has been put away. Each human being needs some corner which is sacred to him or her, which can be left untouched by others, no matter what its state of messiness. It is a personal place of creation, place for solitude, a *sanctum-sanctorum*. A wife needs her sewing space, art studio, or writing corner, or whatever. A husband needs his workshop, home desk, or photographic developing closet where work-in-progress can be left inviolate. If these can be shielded from the public eye so that they don't have to be whisked into tidiness when guests drop in, well and good; but better that friends find some wholesome confusion, overlaid with shavings and ravelings, than that a couple nag each other out of the joy of creative activities in the home.

This brings up the matter of privacy, which should be regarded as among the necessities of life and not among its privileges. There is no man, woman, or child who does not need some opportunity to think his or her own thoughts or do his or her own "do" in his or her own way, without interference or interruption from anyone. Preferably, each needs a place which is absolutely his or her own, yet with housing so expensive, house space seems to grow smaller, especially for the limited budgets of most newlyweds. However, there is usually a way to achieve that which is recognized as valuable. The trap that most young couples fall into is that they settle for *any* space at all where they can be together without external interference. They never dream that they can be an interference *to each other*. Then, some months later, they discover that each is chafing at too much confinement and too little privacy.

"Too much togetherness," one husband wryly complained. "I wish the word had never been adopted as the symbol of family happiness."

The zest of being with a person you love is keenest after an opportunity for separateness. The excitement and thrill lie in the coming back *into* togetherness, the bringing *to* the other the loot of the mind's forays while separate.

There are any number of practical and ingenious ways to achieve privacy, even within a small space. Many couples, for example, have given up their dining room to use as a hobby room, with wall-dividers sectioning off each person's domain. Even more simply, others live and sleep in their living room, using the intended bedroom as their study, divided into two section.

If possible, try to make your first home include at least two rooms. Better a cheaper neighborhood with more space than cramped quarters in a fashionable one.

Some partners in love stumble over a curious snag, which

often they don't recognize for a good many months. They only know that they are becoming more and more tense and short tempered with each other about what seems like nothing at all. This snag is a difference in tempo; in other words, the speed at which they do things. Did you ever try to breathe in exact rhythm with another person? Try it some time, and after a few minutes note how the stress becomes almost unbearable. Yet, partners in love, in their enthusiasm for "togetherness," sometimes try to enforce on themselves, or on each other, this impossible, stress-producing exercise. Ask any farmer how hard it is to match a team of horses, and you will begin to get an idea of what I am talking about.

If you walk fast and he walks slowly, it is folly to try to walk arm-in-arm. My husband, who was an ambler, and I, who am a canterer, were always being brought up short with irritation, on this score. One fine day, he drew a cartoon, which he left on my desk. It was of a long-legged woman streaking down the street with a disgruntled man hailing a taxi. It was captioned, "Keep up with that woman." I got the point. Thereafter, when we took our walks, I learned to enjoy my cantering alone, permitting myself side forays to take up time while he ambled happily, both of us meeting at preplanned places along the way.

If a husband washes dishes with lightning speed and his wife dries them at a snail's pace, she mustn't expect him to stand around chomping at the bit like a restless stallion while she finishes up her part of the job.

My husband and I couldn't make beds together, and there were any number of other tasks we couldn't do together either. We didn't try. When a task demands two persons' efforts, we agreed on who would do what and the task got done amicably.

Some people are such rugged individualists that no one can anticipate what they will do next or how they will do it.

These people are exciting to live with but next to impossible to do a simple chore with. Many households are like that. The partners end up waving merrily to each other across spaces, but better that than cross admonitions to "Hurry up!" or "Slow down!" Because tempo is such a highly individualistic matter, you simply move at your own pace, making ample provision for the pace of the other fellow. But don't try to change anyone's pace, for it has biological roots too deep to tamper with. Outside the army, it just isn't practical.

The same principle is at work in the matter of likes and dislikes in leisure-time activity. You may like to dance. He may hate it. Does this need to interfere with your partnership in love? It does not. Not for one moment do you have to "sacrifice" your enjoyment of dancing, or he to engage upon it against his will. You may find it more socially practical to change the environment for your dance, but dance you may.

He may like to play golf and you don't; but when his golf game is in progress, there is nothing to keep you from taking your sketch pad to the course and meeting him at the nineteenth hole for a joint celebration of your happy day.

On the other hand, you may welcome this free time to get needed chores done so that when he comes home you can both enjoy a bit of relaxation together. The *amount* of time that two people spend together is not a criterion of the intensity or satisfaction in their relationship. It is the quality that counts. One glance of exchanged love, one heart-felt laugh provoked, one word of deep appreciation, one moment of thoughts shared—these are what ripen and sustain a love, not clock hours spent in each other's company.

I haven't heard any recent eulogy on the virtue of the king or queen size bed as a sensitizer of man to wife and vice versa, but I think that there should be one. You hardly know a person at all until you know his or her body in sleep.

The communications of man to woman and woman to man reach unsuspected depths in sleep consciousness. Without words, without sight, beyond reason, the state of well-being of the beloved is understood and nourished through the body radiations of one to the other. Unless you have unusual handicaps, I recommend that you give yourselves the experience of trying this pathway to mutual knowledge and healing.

Friends are the salt of this earth. Like an irridescent background against which the light of your love shines in vari-colored harmonies, friendships reveal you and your partner to each other in ways that could never have been visible otherwise. They call out unsuspected facets of your character which enrich your love in unbounded manner.

My husband and I had a favorite island, the length and breadth of which we had explored. However, when one of our friends guided us to an inlet or a waterfall, we discovered new coves and hidden glens which we didn't know existed. So it is with your partner in love. Familiar as he or she is to you, a treasure trove opens up as he or she exposes himself or herself further in response to others.

Occasionally, deep friendships are frightening to young couples, though they needn't be. The richer each of you is in your friendships, the richer and safer the two of you can be in your mutual relationship.

There are some friends, however, who *do* tend to exclude one partner or the other. These can be temporarily devastating to the odd-man-out. Here is a time when the "in" partner needs to take a strong stand, defining to his (her) friend the inclusive nature of the love partnership. This usually clues the friend to less exclusiveness. I do not mean that all of a person's social or professional acquaintances be brought into the intimate orbit of the family circle or that professional secrets be shared with one's wife, but I do mean that good and deep friends of one partner are wisely told that there are no secrets from the other partner.

Sometimes a male friend feels that a husband will experience a pang of jealousy if his relationship with the wife is known, so he urges her to spare her partner such knowledge. This is nearly always a mistake. If the friend was correct, then it is doubly important for man and wife to talk this out between themselves. Why *need* the husband be jealous? On what is founded his insecurity? His lack of faith? In what way *can* a good friend of either sex take away anything from *either* partner?

I think that it is wise for husbands and wives to go out of their ways to get to know well the close friends of their partners. Once you understand a person; once he or she understands you, it is next to impossible for him or her to exploit or hurt you, and vice versa. The "other" man or "other" woman can only be a threat when there is a closed door between man and wife or when, out of fear, a friendship is driven underground.

Jim was upset because his wife had a woman friend to whom she looked for comfort and understanding in the most intimate details of life. During every crisis, Sylvia turned to Martha, as well as to Jim. "Was this a Lesbian attachment?" worried Jim.

I could assure him that it wasn't. But it became important for Jim to understand what *was* operative in his wife's emotional yearnings. Sylvia had never known a mother, and Martha supplied an answer to this need while Sylvia "lived out" her lost childhood. With compassion and great tenderness, Martha gave Sylvia mother-warmth and mother-love. Presently, as Sylvia's starvation eased, her intense attachment for Martha relaxed into that of a ripe and good friendship, taking its proper place in Jim's and Sylvia's scheme of things. Today Jim and Sylvia welcome Martha warmly whenever she drops in.

I have known many such temporary, but intense relationships to occur in marriages. They are something like the crushes experienced in adolescence, and, like them, need to be treated tenderly. In one partner or the other, some need is felt, some passion awakened, but when fulfilled, the intensity lessens and the friendship assumes comfortable proportions. These relationships need to be understood and not fought, for they are rarely threatening unless driven undercover.

Some of the best experiences a couple can have come about because of friends. Tasks are accomplished in half the time and with twice the pleasure. Food tastes doubly good. Sorrow is lessened, joy is heightened. The agape, or ancient fellowship of love, where persons brought the best of which they were capable to share with each other in a feast of love, has continued to shed its grace on modern couples in love, to this day.

A natural outgrowth of the love of one human being for another is a greater capacity to love all within one's sphere. Love moves out and is increased, not diminished, the more it is given. What starts with love of one, overflows into a world of loving relationships which enrich the giver and the receiver. A partner in love is the biological and spiritual unit for all that is good and creative and at peace in this world.

APPENDIX A

Suggested Readings

Love and Marriage (for the married and about to be married)

Marriage: The Art of Lasting Love. *David R. Mace. Doubleday, 1952.*
Open Marriage: A New Life Style for Couples, *George and Nena O'Neill. Avon, 1973.*
The Art of Loving. *Eric Fromm. Harper & Bros., 1956.*
Love Is Not What You Think. *Jessamyn West. Harcourt, Brace, 1959.*
Intimate Friendships. *James Ramey. Prentice Hall, 1975.*
With This Ring. *Louis H. Burke. McGraw-Hill, 1958.*
The Meaning of Love. *Ashley Montague. Julian Press, 1953.*
Options. *Marcia Seligson. Random House, 1977.*
Beyond Monogamy. *James and Lynn Smith. John Hopkins University Press, 1979.*
Living With Someone Gay. *Don Clark. Celestial Arts, 1977.*
They Lived Happily Ever After. *Leslie C. Bandler. Meta Publications, 1978.*
On Love. *Ortega y Gasset. (translated by Toby Talbot). Meridian Books, 1958.*

The Future of Marriage. *Jessie Bernard. Bantam, 1973.*

Sex Education for Young Children

The Wonderful Story of How You Were Born. *Sidonie Gruenberg. Doubleday, 1952.*
Growing Up. *Karl de Schweinitz. Macmillan, 1945.*
A Baby Is Born. *Milton Levine and Jean Seligman. Golden Press, 1949.*

Sex Education for Teenagers

You. *Sol Gordon. Quadrangle: The New York Times Book Co., 1975.*
Sex Before Marriage. *Eleanor Hamilton, Bantam.* 1969.
Living With Sex—the Student Dilemma. *Richard F. Hettlinger. Seabury Press, 1966.*
Boys and Sex. *Wardell Pomeroy, Ph.D. Delacorte, 1968.*
Girls and Sex. *Wardell Pomeroy, Ph.D. Delacorte, 1968.*
Love and Sex in Plain Language. *Eric Johnson. J. B. Lippincott, 1967.*
Learning About Sex. *Gary Kelly. Barron's Educational Series Rev. ed., 1977.*
Sex With Love. *Eleanor Hamilton, Ph.D. 1978 Beacon Press.*

Sex Education for Adults

An Analysis of Human Sexual Response. *Ruth and Edward Brecher. Little Brown, 1967.*
A Doctor's Marital Guide for Patients. *Bernard Greenblatt M.D. Budlong Press. Distributed through the Milex Corporation, 5915 Northwest Highway, Chicago 31 Illinois. (Available to professional counselors for clients.)*
The Nature and Evolution of Female Sexuality. *Mary Jane Sherfey. Random House, 1972.*
The Art and Science of Love. *Albert Ellis. Lyle Stuart, 1960.*

Appendices

The Pleasure Bond. *Masters and Johnson, Bantam, 1975.*
Illustrated Sex Atlas. *Edited by LeMon Clark, M.D. Health Publications, New York, 1963.*
Control of Birth. *Ernest Havemann and the Staff of Life Magazine, 1967.*
An A B Z of Love. *Inge and Stan Hegeler. Medical Press of New York, 1963.*
How Can I Show That I Love You. *Elise Bowen. Celestial Arts, 231 Adrian Rd., Millbrae, California, 1972.*
Total Orgasm: Advanced Techniques for Increasing Sexual Pleasure. *Jack Rosenberg Random House Bookworks, 1973.*
More Joy of Sex. *Alex Comfort. Simon and Schuster, 1974.*
The Hite Report. *Shere Hite. MacMillan, 1976.*
Getting Clear: Body Work for Women. *Anne Kent Rush, Random House Bookworks, 1973.*
Human Sexual Response. *William Masters and Virginia Johnson. Little Brown and Company, 1966.*
Liberating Masturbation. *Betty Dodson. San Francisco, 1974.*
My Secret Garden. *Nancy Friday. Trident Press, 1973.*
Male Sexual Fantasies. *Stephen Lewis. Ace Books, 1974.*
The Sex Researchers. *Ed Brecher, Specific Press, 1979.*
Catalogue of Sexual Consciousness. *Saul Braun, ed. Grove Press, 1975.*
V.D. *Eric Johnson. Bantam, 1973.*
The Illustrated Manual of Sex Therapy. *Helen Singer Kaplan, Times Books, 1975.*
The New Sex Therapy. *Helen Singer Kaplan. Brunner Mazel, Inc., 1974.*
For Yourself. *Lonnie Barbach. Doubleday, 1975.*
Human Sexual Inadequacy. *Masters and Johnson. Little Brown, 1970.*
Psycho-Dietics: Food As the Key to Emotional Health. *Emanuel Cheraskin. Stein and Day, 1974.*
The Well Body Book. *Hal Bennett and Michael Samuels. Random House, 1973.*

101 Intimate Sexual Problems Answered. Dr. LeMon Clark. Signet, 1967.

Childbirth (for prospective parents)

Birth. *Catherine Milinaire. Crown Publichers, 1971.*
Childbirth Without Fear. *Grantly Dick Read. Harper & Bros., 1944.*
The Natural Childbirth Primer. *Grantly Dick Read. Harper & Bros., 1956.*
Awake and Aware. *Irwin Chabon, M.D. Dell, 1966.*
Thank You Dr. Lamaze. *Majorie Karmel. Dolphin Books, Doubleday, 1959.*
Psychoprophylactic Preparation for Painless Childbirth. *Isidore Bonstein. Grune & Stratton, 1958.*
Six Practical Lessons for an Easier Childbirth. *Elizabeth Bing. Bantam, 1969.*
Mother and Baby Care in Pictures. *Louise Zabriskie. J. B. Lippincott, 1953.*
Conception, Birth, and Contraception. *Robert L. Dickinson and John Sciaria. McGraw Hill.*
Modern Motherhood. *H. M. I. Liley, M.D. Random House, 1967.*
Birth Without Violence. *Frederick Leboyer. Knopf, 1975.*

Child Care and Family Problems

The Womanly Art of Breast Feeding. *LaLeche League, Franklin Park, Ill., 1963.*
One Little Boy. *Dorothy Walter Baruch. Julian Press, 1952.*
Baby and Child Care. *Benjamin Spock, M.D. Duell, Sloan & Pearce, 1946.*
The Growing Family. *Edited by Maxwell Stewart. Harper & Bros., 1956.*
The Problems of Family Life. *Edited by Maxwell Stewart. Harper & Bros., 1956.*

When a Family Needs Therapy. *Gina Ogden and Anne Zevin, Beacon Press, 1976.*
Films—Available Thru: Planned Parenthood
                        National Sex Forum, 1523 Franklin St., San Francisco
                        Siecus
                        Eacoa
Vibrators—Eves Garden, West 57 St., NY City, NY
       Most drugstores

APPENDIX B

Suggested Literature that May Deepen and Widen Your Appreciation of the Many Faces of Love.

Centuries before the modern psychologic search for the meaning and creation of love, artists struggled to distil its essence. As a sensitive novelist once said to me, "All great works of fiction are involved with love in some form."

Certainly a novel can educate you emotionally as very few technical books can. Since a partnership in love is primarily a partnership requiring emotional development, I suggest that you expose yourself to the rich gifts that our artists have laid at your feet.

In compiling this list, I called upon a number of friends to select from their literary heritage those books that had made some real contribution to their own understanding of love. A few submitted titles that portrayed the misery that accompanies the failure to love. Many of the selections are unfamiliar to me; others I would not have chosen. However, these are all choices of men and women of discriminating taste, whose own capacity to love richly I

Appendices

admire. Those titles that have meant the most to me in my own development, I have starred.

Because many of these books achieved popularity and were reprinted in paperback editions, a few under several different reprints, I have not attempted to list the publishers and their dates of issue. Most of these will be on the shelves of any public library. I suggest, of course, that you ask your bookseller to show you the best available editions. The paperbacks are low in cost, but you may want the regular hardbound editions for your home library.

A Death in the Family	*James Agee*
Young Love	*Johannes Allen*
Emma	*Jane Austen*
Cousin Bette	*Honoré de Balzac*
Eugénie Grandet	*Honoré de Balzac*
The Mandarins	*Simone de Beauvoir*
The Death of the Heart	*Elizabeth Bowen*
To the North	*Elizabeth Bowen*
A Room at the Top	*John Braine*
Jane Eyre	*Charlotte Brontë*
Wuthering Heights	*Emily Brontë*
*The Good Earth	*Pearl Buck*
A Change of Heart	*Michel Butor*
A Lost Lady	*Willa Cather*
Lucy Gayheart	*Willa Cather*
My Mortal Enemy	*Willa Cather*
Cheri	*Colette*
The Last of Cheri	*Colette*
My Mother's House	*Colette*
The Ripening Seed	*Colette*
The Vagabond	*Colette*
Adolphe	*Benjamin Constant*
The Red Notebook	*Benjamin Constant*
Forever	*Mildred Cram*
The Citadel	*A. J. Cronin*
Sappho	*Alphonse Daudet*

The Constant Image	Marcia Davenport
The Breeze From Camelot	Vina Delmar
Seven Gothic Tales	Isak Dinesen
Magnificent Obsession	Lloyd C. Douglas
Crime and Punishment	Fyodor Dostoyevsky
An American Tragedy	Theodore Dreiser
Sister Carrie	Theodore Dreiser
Camille	Alexander Dumas, Fils.
*My Life	Isadora Duncan
Clea	Lawrence Durrell
Justine	Lawrence Durrell
Mountolive	Lawrence Durrell
Balthazar	Lawrence Durrell
Middlemarch	George Eliot
Requiem for a Nun	William Faulkner
The Wild Palms	William Faulkner
Cimarron	Edna Ferber
Show Boat	Edna Ferber
Tender Is the Night	F. Scott Fitzgerald
The Beautiful and the Damned	F. Scott Fitzgerald
Madame Bovary	Gustave Flaubert
Sentimental Education	Gustave Flaubert
Love Is a Bridge	Charles Bracelen Flood
The Africa Queen	C. S. Forester
The Good Soldier	Ford Madox Ford
Howards End	E. M. Forster
The Longest Journey	E. M. Forster
Where Angels Fear to Tread	E. M. Forster
The Wanderer	Henri Alain-Fournier
Claudia	Rose Franken
Another Claudia	Rose Franken
The Story of Gabrielle	Catherine Gabrielson
*The Broken Wings	Kahlil Gibran
Madeleine	André Gide
Strait Is the Gate	André Gide
The Immoralist	André Gide
The School for Wives, Robert and Genevive	André Gide

Appendices

Barren Ground	*Ellen Glasgow*
The Lying Days	*Nadine Gordimer*
Close to Colette	*Maurice Goudeket*
*Winged Pharoah	*Joan Grant*
End of the Affair	*Graham Green*
The Young Lovers	*Julian Halevy*
The Well of Loneliness	*Radclyffe Hall*
Growth of the Soil	*Knut Hamsun*
Far From the Madding Crowd	*Thomas Hardy*
The Mayor of Casterbridge	*Thomas Hardy*
The Scarlet Letter	*Nathaniel Hawthorne*
A Farewell to Arms	*Ernest Hemingway*
For Whom the Bell Tolls	*Ernest Hemingway*
The Eighth Day of the Week	*Marek Hlasko*
*Green Mansions	*W. H. Hudson*
Home From the Hill	*William Humphrey*
The Golden Bowl	*Henry James*
Wings of the Dove	*Henry James*
Letters to Milena	*Franz Kafka*
Snow Country	*Yasunari Kawabata*
The Greek Passion	*Nikos Kazantzakis*
Three Came Home	*Agnes Newton Keith*
Dangerous Acquaintances	*Choderlos de Laclos*
Lady Chatterley's Lover	*D. H. Lawrence*
Sons and Lovers	*D. H. Lawrence*
*The Man Who Died	*D. H. Lawrence*
The Rainbow	*D. H. Lawrence*
Women in Love	*D. H. Lawrence*
Dusty Answer	*Rosamond Lehmann*
A Hero of Our Times	*Mikhail Lermontov*
Arrowsmith	*Sinclair Lewis*
Dodsworth	*Sinclair Lewis*
Raintree Country	*Ross Lockridge, Jr.*
Aphrodite	*Pierre Louÿs*
Evangeline	*Henry Wadsworth Longfellow*
The Watch That Ends the Night	*Hugh McLennan*
The Assistant	*Bernard Malamud*

The Beloved Returns	*Thomas Mann*
Betrothed	*Alessandro Manzoni*
Nectar in a Sieve	*Kamala Markandaya*
Of Human Bondage	*Somerset Maugham*
September Roses	*André Maurois*
They Came Like Swallows	*William Maxwell*
The Heart is a Lonely Hunter	*Carson McCullers*
Persian Adventure	*Anne Sinclair Mehdevi*
Strangers	*Albert Memmi*
The Sound of Waves	*Yukio Mishima*
Gone with the Wind	*Margaret Mitchell*
*Sayonara	*James Michener*
*Fires of Spring	*James Michener*
The Luck of Ginger Coffey	*Brian Moore*
Héloïse and Abélard	*George Moore*
Peter Abelard	*Helen Waddell*
Leave Cancelled	*Nicholas Monsarrat*
Bitter Honeymoon	*Alberto Moravia*
Conjugal Love	*Alberto Moravia*
The Price of Salt	*Claire Morgan*
The Tale of Genji	*Lady Murasaki*
Katherine Mansfield's Letters to John Middleton Murry	*John M. Murry*
Grateful to Life and Death	*R. K. Narayan*
Portrait of Jennie	*Robert Nathan*
Chiara	*Gene d'Olive*
Manon Lescaut	*Abbé Prevost*
Swann's Way	*Marcel Proust*
Devil in the Flesh	*Raymond Radiguet*
The Sojourner	*Marjorie Kinnan Rawlings*
A Time to Love and a Time to Die	*Erich Maria Ramarque*
Three Comrades	*Erich Maria Remarque*
Jealousy	*Alain Robbe-Crillet*
The Time of Man	*Elizabeth Madox Roberts*
Warrior's Rest	*Christiane Rochefort*
*Thursday My Love	*Robert Rimmer*
The Harrod Experiment	*Robert Rimmer*

The Unfaithful Wife	Jules Roy
Nine Stories	J. D. Salinger
Portrait of Zelide	Geoffrey Scott
A Tree Grows in Brooklyn	Betty Smith
Homecoming	C. P. Snow
On Love	Stendhal
The Red and the Black	Stendhal
*The Crock of Gold	James Stephens
Elizabeth and Essex	Lytton Strachey
A Many Splendored Thing	Han Suyin
Vanity Fair	William Makepeace Thackeray
Bridge to the Sun	Gwen Terasaki
Not as a Stranger	Morton Thompson
Anna Karenina	Leo Tolstoy
War and Peace	Leo Tolstoy
Amelie in Love	Henri Troyat
Amelie and Pierre	Henri Troyat
A House of Gentlefolk	Ivan Turgenev
First Love	Ivan Turgenev
Rudin	Ivan Turgenev
Smoke	Ivan Turgenev
Kristin Lavransdatter	Sigrid Undset
Mastro-Don Gesualdo	Giovanni Verga
Winter Wheat	Mildred Walker
The Enemy Camp	Jerome Weidman
And the Bridge Is Love	Alma Mahler Werfel
Death of a Man	Lael Tucker Wertenbaker
Ethan Frome	Edith Wharton
The Age of Innocence	Edith Wharton
Woman of Andros	Thornton Wilder
The Web and the Rock	Thomas Wolfe
Mrs. Dalloway	Virginia Woolf

I suggest also that after you have scanned this list, you immediately make up your own list. Many of the titles here may have special meaning for you. However, since each of us has, to some extent at least, a different range of experiences, you may have an entirely different list of books. These may certainly be of value to your friends, and, in the instance of ministers and other counsellors, to those who come to them for guidance. In any case, the effort to draw up such a personal list will cause you to reflect upon the richest resources in your reading and perhaps even astonish you that books, as they inevitably do, should have formed so many of your reactions on love and its manifold aspects.

Index

Anger: blocking of love by, 53; control of, 53; moodiness resulting from, 90; muscular tensions from, 50, 82, 83, 84, 113, 114; releasing of, 50, 51, 52, 58, 59, 84, 113; repression of, 23, 29, 50
Anxiety: against pleasure, 25, 98, 111, 112, 131, 181; childbirth, 141; contractions against, 25; contributing to sexual dysfunction, 126, 127; pregnancy, 141, 142; respiratory symptoms of, 65; sexual, 141, 142; tensions, 31, 65, 66, 87
Appreciation: blocked, 35, 59; of family, 160, 161, 175; giving of, 35, 59, 75, 195, 196, 197, 198, 199; need for, 197, 198, 199; receiving of, 35, 196; of sexual structure, 126
Autoeroticism. *See* Genital play

Birth control: contraception, 137; and economic considerations, 135, 136, 137; and family planning, 132, 133, 134, 135, 136; and marital happiness, 132, 133; sources for education in, 137
Birth impressions, effects of: environmental, 20, 21, 22, 23; on infant, 20, 21, 22, 23; on mother, 21, 22
Blocking, holding in: of appreciation, 59, 60; in breathing, 55, 56; in communication, 71; of complaints, 58; of emotional expression, 81, 82; of feelings, 54, 55, 58; of love, 53, 58; of tears, 53, 85, 86; of understanding, 57, 60, 72, 73
Books recommended. *See* Appendices, 211–22
Breathing (communication), related to: adult, 25, 26, 65, 66, 71; childbirth, 55; infant, 24, 25; repressed feelings, 25, 55, 57; sexual pleasure, 24, 96, 113, 114, 131; tension, 24, 25, 55, 56, 65; technique of complete exhalation, 56

Cleanliness, personal hygiene, 202, 203
Communication: by breathing, 24, 25, 71; interpreting, 53, 69, 70, 72, 73, 84, 85, 92; in moodiness, 79, 80, 81, 86, 87, 88, 92; by movement, 69; by muscular tension, 82, 83, 84; need for, 88, 89; nonverbal, 64, 65, 66, 197, 198, 199, 207, 208; by odor, 68, 201, 202, 203; in sharing experiences, 62, 63, 74, 75; by touch, 30, 34, 65, 67, 95, 96, 104; verbal, 64, 65, 70, 71, 74, 75, 76, 95, 98, 99, 101
Complaints, criticism: analyzing, 59; blocking of, 58; "unloading" of, 58

Daydreams: aspirations in, 133, 134, 151, 152, 157, 181

223

Dreams, nightmares: sharing of, 77, 78

Emotions: awareness of tone in, 107; correcting false conclusions of, 47, 57, 58, 71, 72, 73; definition of, 112; healing wounded, 45, 46, 47, 48, 49, 93; helping the maturing of, 74; in moodiness, 81, 82; painful, effects of, 54, 55; pleasant, effects of, 20, 41, 44, 50, 54; repressed, effects of, 22, 23, 24, 36, 50, 53, 54, 81, 82, 83, 84, 86, 87, 101
Environment, effects of, 22, 25, 203, 204, 205, 206
Erogenous zones: anal, 30, 31, 32; breasts, 146; genital, 27, 28, 31, 32, 105, 107; oral, 28, 29

Fear: body tension in, 87; of emotional expression, 83, 85, 113, 114; in infants, 23; in moodiness, 79; of pregnancy, 133, 141, 142; of rejection, 23, 36, 91, 99; in sexual relations, 69, 122, 123, 124, 125
Frustration. *See* Emotions, repressed

Genital play: in adult, 27, 28, 105, 107; in infant, 27, 31, 32, 111; in marriage, 27; use of lubricant in, 105; use of vibrator in, 105, 106, 112
Givingness: of appreciation, 35, 59, 60, 61, 195, 196; as child, 33, 34; of healing by love, 47, 48, 49, 93, 186
Guilt Feelings: about emotional reactions, 37, 38; about parents, 162; about pregnancy, 140, 141; about reaching for pleasures, 40, 41; because of rejection, 23, 24; about sex, 101

Jealousy: of mate's friends, 90, 208, 209, 210; of mate's other personal relationships, 194; of mate's work, 176, 177; of mate towards baby, 146

Love: determining, 16, 17; growth in, 19, 59, 93, 149, 150, 161, 190; healings of emotional wounds, 47, 48, 49, 93; image of, 38; longings of, 18, 19, 43, 44, 45, 46, 145; strengthening of, 62, 63, 64, 74, 93, 161, 181

Masters and Johnson: treatment for premature ejaculation, 129, 130; treatment for vaginismus, 117, 118
Masturbation. *See* Genital play
Money: attitude toward, 147; budgeting of, 152, 153, 157; clarifying goals, 151, 152, 153, 157; dependence on parents for, 169, 173; management of, 150, 151, 157; mutual trust regarding, 149; neuroses about, 154, 155, 156; requirements for marriage, 152, 153, 154, 155; spending, as partners, 149, 150, 157
Moodiness: because of lack of sexual stimulation, 99; in damaged self-feeling, 90, 91; emotional expressions of, 86, 87, 88; silence because of, 79, 80; tension communication in, 80, 82, 83; in undermining of trust, 91, 92; in unexpressed angers, 82, 83, 84, 90

Needs: anal, 30, 31, 32; appreciation, 196, 197, 198, 199; approval, 22, 30, 47, 197, 198; communication, 88, 89; emotional release, 50, 51, 52, 53, 58, 84, 85, 86, 87; emotional support during pregnancy, 143, 144, 145; genital, 27, 28, 31, 32; oral, 28, 29, 30; privacy, 205, 206; sexual, 114, 115; trust, 88, 89, 91, 92, 93, 149

Odors: as communication, 68, 69, 202, 203; magnetic, 68, 201, 202; offensive, 68, 69, 202

Parents: appreciation of, 171, 172, 175; clarifying goals to, 174, 175; dependence on, 159, 169, 173; influence of, 158, 159, 160, 161, 171, 184; in-laws, 162, 172, 174; living with, 173, 174;

Index 225

opinions of, 158, 160, 161, 162; traditions of, 158, 159, 160; weaning from, 166, 168, 197
Pregnancy: childbirth anxiety in, 21, 141, 142; contraception against, 137; desire for, 132, 133; economic considerations in, 135, 136, 137; emotional support during, 143, 144, 145; fear of, 133; personality changes during, 139, 140, 141; planning, 133, 134, 135, 136; premarital, 138, 139, 140; resistance to, 133; sexual adjustment during, 141, 142; training for, 137, 138, 142, 143

Reaching (for satisfactions): as adult, 40, 41, 42, 43, 44; fear of, 23, 24, 25, 40, 41, 97; as infant, 22, 23, 24, 29
Rejection (feelings of): from criticism, 58, 59; because of expressed emotion, 36; because of false emotional conclusions, 47, 57, 58, 72, 73; of self, 22, 23, 24, 25, 30, 34, 90, 91; because of sexual denial, 97, 98
Religion: differences of, in marriage, 189, 194; inherited rituals of, 125, 127, 189, 190; sharing spiritual awareness of, 188, 190, 193, 194

Sexual artistry: erotic literature and films in, 102, 103, 105; foreplay in, 103, 104, 105; massaging in, 96; oral, 103; orgasm, achieving through, 103, 104, 105; patterns of stimulation in, 119, 120; petting in, 98, 101; sexual energy levels in, 100, 101, 103; timing in, 118, 119; touch communication in, 95, 96, 103; variety in, 102, 103; use of speech in, 95, 98, 99, 101
Sexual communication: accomplished in, 97; beginner in, 97; healing touch approval in, 95, 96; healthy, 94, 95; verbal 95, 98, 99, 101
Sexual dysfunction: alcohol as contributing to, 126, 127; anger as contributing to, 113; anxiety as contributing to, 126, 127; breathing to relieve, 131; erectile ability in, 124; fungus infections as contributing to, 120, 121; levels of sexual inadequacy as contributing to, 109, 110; male impotence as contributing to, 117, 124, 125, 127, 128; muscular tension as contributing to, 113, 114, 117, 118; orgasm, achieving in, 109, 110, 112, 113, 114, 115, 119, 120, 121; patterns of stimulation as an aid in combating, 119, 120; pleasure anxiety as contributing to, 111, 112, 131; premature ejaculation as contributing to, 118, 128, 129; releasing of tensions to combat, 113, 114; sex fears as contributing to, 122, 123, 124, 125; sexual frigidity as contributing to, 109, 110; timing as a deterrent to, 118, 119, vaginismus as contributing to, 115–18; woman as aggressor as deterrent to, in male, 125, 126
Sexual fulfillment: autoeroticism in, 107; contraception in, 137; foreplay for, 103, 104, 105; imagination as key for, 105; lack of desire for, 101, 102; lack of interest for, 102; orgasm, achieving in, 28, 97, 98, 100, 101, 103, 104, 105, 106, 107, 108, 114, 115, 119, 120, 121; petting for, 98, 101; proper breathing for increased pleasure in, 96, 113, 114; release of creative energy for, 107, 108; variety as contributing to, 102, 103
Sharing: appreciation, 195, 196; aspirations, 133, 134, 151, 152; communication, 33, 62, 63, 74, 75; complaints, criticism, 57, 58, 59; dreams, 76, 77; experience, 47, friends, 90, 160, 207, 208, 209, 210; home decorating, 203, 204; jealousy, 90; privacy, 205, 206; recreation, 207; religion, 192, 193, 194; tempo, 205, 206; woman as the aggressor in, 99, 100

Tension, causes of: anger, 50; anxiety, 25, 31, 87; fear, 87; moodiness, 80; repressed emotions, 50, 54, 82, 83, 84, 113, 114; repressed tears, 53, 86, 87
Tension, communicated through: manner of breathing, 24, 25, 55, 56; muscular contraction, 23, 82, 83, 84, 85, 112, 113, 117, 118

Trust: in your own feelings, 36, 37, 38; in mate's dependability, 92, 93; of mate in money matters, 149; in mate's understanding, 88, 89

Work: appreciation of, 59, 60, 182, 183, 184, 185, 187; clarifying goals of, 151, 152, 157; jealousy of, 176, 177; objections to wife working, 182–87; partnership with mate, 177, 178, 181; rewards, pleasures of, 178, 179, 180, 181; significance of, 176, 177, 178